Sport Climbing in the Santa Monicas

The Climbing Guide to the Santa Monica Mountains

2nd Edition

D1729070

Diana Jew on **Ground Zero** 12a** at Malibu Creek. ©*Perri Nguyen Photo.*

Sport Climbing in the Santa Monicas

The Climbing Guide to the Santa Monica Mountains

By Louie Anderson
2nd Edition

**SOUTHERN CALIFORNIA
CLIMBING GUIDES VOL. 1**

MAXIMVS PRESS

Maximus Press
P.O.Box 3952
Mammoth Lakes, CA 93546
Phone & Fax: 760-387-1013
E-mail: smlewis@qnet.com
MAXIMVS PRESS http://maximuspress.com

SPORT CLIMBING IN
THE SANTA MONICAS
The Climbing Guide to the Santa Monica Mountains

BY LOUIE ANDERSON
2ND EDITION

SOUTHERN CALIFORNIA CLIMBING GUIDES VOL. 1

June 2003 Second Edition
ISBN 0-9676116-6-0
Copyright © 2003 Maximus Press

Front Cover Photo: Jeff Truman on **The Stand** 13a****. ©*Perri Nguyen Photo.*
Left Back Cover Photo: Doniel Drazin on **Filth Pig** 13b***. ©*Perri Nguyen Photo.*
Right Back Cover Photo: Diana Jew on **Skeezer Pleaser** 11b****. ©*Perri Nguyen Photo*
All Topos and uncredited Photos by the author.

Printed in Canada

To all the climbers who frequent the Santa Monicas. Your enjoyment makes all the work worthwhile and rewarding.

ACKNOWLEDGMENTS

N o guidebook is the result of a single individual's efforts. This guide is no exception. The following people in particular have made contributions in one form or another:

Matt Callender—For always making himself available to check out the new stuff and for input on grades and quality ratings.

Pierre Daigle—The workhorse. Pierre was always up for climbing, bolting, whatever... with little or no notice. While his name does not appear too often in this guide, rest assured that Pierre was very responsible for much of what you see represented here.

Doniel Drazin—My partner in crime. Doniel remotivated me in a big way when he began climbing at Echo. The continued development of that crag and the addition of so many wonderful, moderate routes has been instigated to a great degree by Doniel.

Steve Edwards—Fellow developer and a personal motivator for years. Steve is largely responsible for the climbing in and around Santa Barbara, and his 2000 guidebook brought the Echo Cliffs and Boney Bluff routes to a larger audience.

Mark Fekkes—Mark was always there, ready to try the new routes, and make them look easy.

Craig Fry, Dave Katz and Troy Mayr—Prior to this guide, and Steve's 2000 guide, all past climbing info on the Santa Monicas was presented by these guys. Thanks for spreading the word!

Dean Goolsby—Dean was involved in the early stages of both Echo Cliffs and Boney Bluff and was a constant source of motivation. An excellent photographer, the pictures Dean brought back from his days climbing there showed members of the local community what the Santa Monicas had to offer.

Eric Hinds—The local. I first met Eric through a mutual climbing friend. When we began developing Echo Cliffs, I learned that he lived mere miles from the crag. Eric was a consistent face at the crag in the early years. Thanks for the belays.

Evan Jones, Jim Richardson, Karen Rogel and all the other rangers and officials for their continued support of climbing activities in their jurisdictions.

Joe Kristy—Teamed with John Long, Joe has made a huge impact in recent developments at Malibu Creek and elsewhere in the Santa Monicas. Thank you for your hard work.

Bill Leventhal—Bill has climbed in the Santa Monicas from day one and is responsible for a lot of the early development in the area.

Marty Lewis—For helping to take a ton of information and transform it into an attractive and effective guidebook. A longtime friend and THE man behind the Owens River Gorge.

John Long—LARGO. From holding my rope and making me try his ludicrous boulder problems when I was just another kid in Yosemite until now, John has been a constant source of inspiration. His help with the Malibu Creek and Backbone sections of this guide have made them immeasurably better. Thank you also for writing the Foreword.

Mike Maki—National Park Service Ranger when Echo was originally shut down. Mike's attitude and efforts helped to address concerns and to get the crag opened to climbing again. Thank you for this, and for helping to open the lines of communication between the Park Service and the climbing community.

Jack Marshall—One of the most prolific new route developers in Southern California, Jack was a very big part of the initial development at Echo Cliffs.

Traci Marx—Who could ever doubt the impact of a smile and a happy demeanor? Thanks for infecting us all.

Chris Murray—From the first time, my days climbing with Chris have been rewarding. While other commitments have limited his time on the rock lately, Chris is still a big source of support and a great partner.

Perri Nguyen—For the wonderful photos and making himself available to help me fill in the blanks.

Matt Oliphant—Matt has been climbing at Malibu Creek as long as anyone and some of the best routes there have his name on them.

Jeff Willis—The man with the vision. I'm sure that the Backbone areas would have been developed sooner or later, but Jeff's initial vision of the area's potential motivated us all and redirected our attention to what could be.

All who have bolted and helped to develop climbing areas here and abroad. Few climbers realize the massive amount of time, energy and money you have donated to broaden our climbing options. Thank you one and all!

And finally to *Carla, Kayla and Madison*; my wonderful wife and daughters, for your love and support. Thank you for tolerating my absences: physically (while gone climbing and gathering information) and mentally (while sitting in front of the computer working on this guide). I love you.

TABLE OF CONTENTS

FOREWORD

Malibu Creek State Park and the Echo Cliffs area are only 30 min. apart, and both fall within the greater Santa Monica Mountain range. In terms of the number of routes and the wide variety of individual cliffs within each locale, the Malibu/Echo Cliffs combo presents Los Angeles based climbers with one of the richest hometown sport climbing areas in America. And to be sure, most every route in the Santa Monicas is a bolt protected, clip-and-go sport climb. The standard rack for either area of fifteen quickdraws and a rope covers you for hundreds of routes.

New route activity first started at Malibu in the mid '80s, concurrent with the sport climbing revolution. The ever popular Apes Wall became a top-rope destination featuring dozens of fifty-foot climbs of the 5.9 to 5.12 variety. The large boulders and streambed walls further down the canyon yielded dozens of exciting climbs, including Urban Struggle, which is the gateway into 5.12 for many So Cal climbers. Malibu exploration ebbed and flowed for a decade, ground to a stop in the '90s, and then picked back up in 2000, with areas such as Mt. Gorgeous and the canyon below Century Lake providing stacks of new routes. Owing to the central location, easy approach (25 minutes by foot from the parking lot), and the wide variety of climbs, Malibu remains a perfect day crag, with six distinct areas and enough routes to climb yourself to smithereens. Malibu even lends itself to half-day use. Due to the high concentration of routes in a given area, a couple hours at any of the popular locations (The Ghetto, Mt. Gorgeous, Century Lake Canyon, et al) is sufficient to draw a commendable pump. Exploration continues at Malibu with folks tromping far and wide searching for the next Great Cliffside, and future editions of this guide will no doubt feature scores of additional routes at presently unknown crags.

The popular Backbone Area spans a fairly broad piece of real estate and currently sports a half dozen or so individual venues, the most fashionable and established being the various faces and walls making up Echo Cliffs. A leisurely and glorious 30-45 minute hike along a largely dead-flat nature trail and you're ready to rope up and have at hundreds of sport climbs, from a scattering of 5.9 warm up routes to the bleakest pocket pulling imaginable.

Staggering labor has gone into developing Echo Cliffs, and visitors will be grateful if not amazed by the cliffside trails, re-bar ladders, anti-erosion terraces, plank benches, and the sheer quantity of bolts spangled on the over one hundred and fifty routes. The beginner will find rather slim pickings, for these walls are steep to overhanging and the holds and pockets good enough, but spare. For the 5.10 climber, however, Echo is heaven. And with virtually a hundred routes at 5.11 to 5.14, advanced climbers could spend years at the area and never exhaust the potential.

See Page 83

Bob Passerini on **Hijacked** 12b**** at Echo Cliffs.

For those willing to hike a little further, other crags within the Backbone Area offer no crowds and a wide array of climbing experiences. For the super hardman, check out Boney Bluff. For a great work out, visit the Hueco Wall and try and climb all the routes in a day (roughly a dozen from 5.9 to 5.11b). Looking for a rush, check out Mt. Olympus, tighten up the sack and cast off on vertical to overhanging cobbles. And for a view second to none, spend a day at Top Hat, where directly below the cliffs, the Boney Peak buttress (highest in the area) plunges thousands of feet into a green valley spilling toward the flat blue Pacific, mere miles below. Boney, Hueco Wall, Pico Raquelita, Olympus, and Top Hat were developed as "destination areas," meaning each has sufficient routes to keep a fit climber busy for an entire day, or in the case of Boney Bluff, a lifetime.

Three other areas covered in this book, and lying just off the Pacific include Point Mugu, Point Dume (pronounced Doom), and the J. Paul Pebble.

I'm not sure when climbing first started at Point Mugu, but for years, when driving along the Pacific Coast Highway between L.A. and Ventura; folks have seen the large slab and twenty-five foot high, graffiti-splattered boulder, riven with nearly a dozen vertical cracks, that sits mere feet off the highway. A smattering of small boulder problems and isolated solo slabs round out this area. Yosemite-trained trad climbers will feast on the graffiti boulder, soloing up the plethora of 25-foot 5.10 cracks without pause. Sport climbers, less familiar with running out the rope on rattler jams, will relish a top-rope, which is easily arranged. While Point Mugu is hardly worth a trip for its own sake, it's certainly worth pulling over and pulling down if you should be driving past. The cracks are a blast, and the ocean view is sublime.

Point Dume features a sixty-foot slab with a handful of bolt protected routes in the 5.7-5.9 range (including the classic 5.6 arete), and around the corner, on the ocean side of the rock, several top-rope problems right up to mid 5.12 can be arranged. The slab, which rises right out of the sand at waters edge, is a favorite backdrop for car commercials, and is an excellent beginner's area. When motivation is low, the weather is hot and the waves good, adventurous climbers can be seen alternating between laps on the wall and exciting junkets of body-surfing the pounding breakers for which Zuma Beach is renowned. But to aspiring body surfers—beware of the wicked shore break! More folks break their necks here than at any other beach in California.

The J. Paul Pebble, located on the beach just below the original J. Paul Getty museum, is nothing more than a twenty-five foot high, conglomerate dirt clod. But since climbers have been cocking around on this rock for decades, you'll have to stop sometime and have a look at the handful of solo routes (there are no reliable top-rope anchors) on the overhanging side. Most feature grievous pebble pinching (up to V8) and are guaranteed to scare the crap out of everyone rash enough to climb them. Depending on the tide, jagged boulders are sometimes littering the base. Don't try these problems till the tide shifts and the sand fills back in. Falls are to be expected, and you'll want the sand landing to avoid a train wreck.

These are just a few of the areas covered in this guide. The Santa Monica Mountains are rife with rock and the following pages will open up a whole new world to Southern California climbers.

Tireless pioneer Louie Anderson has established many of the routes in this guide, and has climbed most all of the others. Louie is the only person qualified to write this guidebook with the accuracy it deserves, and is surely the only person who would take on such a huge project and actually see it through. The debt local and visiting climbers have to Louie for his contributions will only be clear in the following years, and by that time Louie will be called on for another edition to this guide; for new routes continue to go up.

Happy climbing!
—John Long

PREFACE

My first experience in the Santa Monicas came as a bouldering excursion to Malibu Creek with some of my friends from Stoney Point in 1982. That was before the sport climbing revolution and before Malibu saw its first bolts (other than the monster rigging bars on top of the Apes wall). It was a wonderful playground, full of options; however it was a little far from home and other than a few return trips around that time I stayed away until the development of The Ghetto in 1991.

To be honest, I never gave much thought to the Santa Monicas beyond Malibu Creek. Perhaps because I didn't realize just how much area (and rock) was to be found between the 101 freeway and the Pacific. My further education came through the eyes of Jeff Willis. Jeff first took me out to some of the Backbone areas in 1994, eager to show off some of the areas he had found. I must admit that I was amazed at the sheer volume of rock in the area. Echo Cliffs and Boney Bluff were the initial areas to be developed, and both were "discovered" by Jeff. While I have continued to climb, and occasionally bolt, elsewhere the vast majority of my climbing time has been spent in the Santa Monicas since that first trip with Jeff. It has been great to see the transformation of the original areas over the last few years. What were once crags visited only by a small handful of climbers have now become quite popular.

As climbing has continued to rise in popularity, several minor crags have popped up all over the Santa Monicas. Where the first edition of this guide focused only on the Echo Cliffs and Boney Bluff—I have made the effort in this edition to cover all of the previously unpublished areas, as well as updating information to the original areas and to the ever popular Malibu Creek State Park. As more of Southern California's climbing community discovers the wonderful climbing options to be found in the Santa Monicas, I can only imagine what the next edition of this guide might look like.

Have fun and be safe!
—Louie Anderson
June, 2003

See Page 116

Aron Couzens on **Conspiracy** 12a**** at The Lookout.

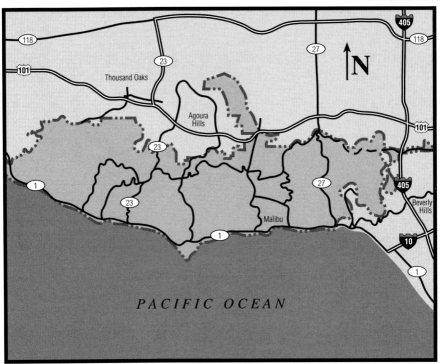

CHAPTER 1

INTRODUCTION

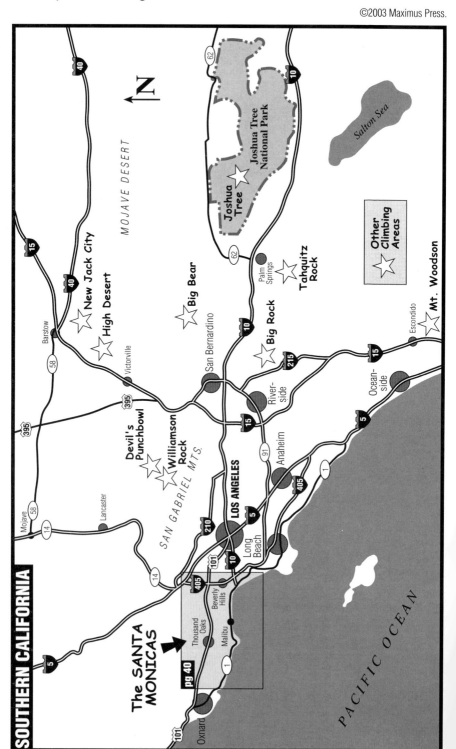

INTRODUCTION

Congratulations! You are examining the latest edition of the first guidebook devoted to the Santa Monica Mountains. This book has been painstakingly researched for *your* enjoyment. Please read the entire introduction.

Where are the Santa Monicas?

The Santa Monica Mountains are located in Southern California, west of Los Angeles, and run between Beverly Hills and Oxnard. The Pacific Coast Hwy. (1) and the Ventura Fwy. (101) provide access to the range.

Driving Times (in hours):

Phoenix 8.5	Las Vegas 5	San Diego 3
Joshua Tree 3.5	Tahquitz Rock 3	Williamson Rock 1.5

Climate

The season at all of the areas within this guide is somewhat the same due to their close proximity. Temperatures are most enjoyable during the fall, winter and spring; but climbing is still possible during the summer.

Winter days can be quite cold and sometimes wet, so be prepared with a sweatshirt, fleece or other warm clothing; and possibly some lightweight rain gear if the weather or forecast looks threatening. Several of the areas offer steep enough terrain to allow for climbing and/or shelter during a sudden rain. On the most bitterly cold mornings (often the best time for hard redpoint attempts) either a heat pack thrown in your chalkbag or pocket, or a small propane fueled heater dish can make things considerably more pleasant.

Summer temperatures can either be quite comfortable or oppressively hot, but seldom anything in between. Throughout the guide, information is supplied as to when specific cliffs are in the shade and most areas offer multidirectionally facing cliffs such that shady climbing is almost always attainable. During the hottest weeks of summer, climbers will certainly want to follow the shade when selecting routes and it's a good idea to throw your water bottles in the freezer a few days before climbing. The steady melt of the frozen water throughout the day will keep you supplied with refreshingly cool water on even the hottest of days. If for some reason the ice is not melting quickly enough to match the pace of your thirst, simply lay the bottle in the direct sun for a few moments and you'll be set. On the hottest of days be sure to pack enough water to prevent dehydration and be sure that your partners do the same. Another concern during the summer months is exposure to the sun. Be prepared by carrying and using an appropriate level of sunscreen to match your body's skin type.

Amenities

The majority of the climbing areas in the Santa Monica Mountains are conveniently located and approached by driving through very developed communities. As such, the regular assortment of fast food, convenience, coffee and liquor establishments are all readily available. Due to this fact, this guide will only highlight a few of the local favorites that might be a little different from the norm, or that are exceptional in their offerings.

The area is known for its seafood restaurants and you will be assaulted with uncountable options along these lines as you drive down the Pacific Coast Highway. Remember that this is a beach community and that even though some of the restaurants listed below (and others found in the immediate area) might be "classier" establishments, that in all but the most exclusive—casual dress is allowed and considered the norm. Because of this you can go straight from the crag to a top-notch meal with only minimal clean up required.

Please refer to the Santa Monica Mountains Amenities and Camping Map on page 20 for rough relationships of these establishments to individual climbing areas.

Camping

From Topanga State Park to Point Mugu State Park there are a variety of campgrounds. Please refer to the Santa Monica Mountains Amenities and Camping Map on page 20 for the campground locations.

©2003 Maximus Press.

Campground Information	Flush Toilets	Showers	Pets	Fee	Phone	Reservations
Leo Carrillo State Park Hike and Bike	●	●	●	$1	805-488-5223	None Availible
Leo Carrillo State Park Canyon Family	●	●	●	$12	805-488-5223	800-444-7275
Big Sycamore Canyon Hike and Bike	●	●		$1	805-488-5223	None Availible
Big Sycamore Canyon Family Camp	●	●	●	$12	805-488-5223	800-444-7275
Thornhill Broome Family Camp			●	$7	805-488-5223	800-444-7275
Malibu Creek Family Camp	●	●	●	$12	818-880-0367	800-444-7275
Musch Camp Backcountry Hike-in	●			$1	310-455-2465	None Availible

See Page 145

Tony Sartin on **Ghetto Blaster** 13a***** at Malibu Creek. ©*Perri Nguyen Photo.*

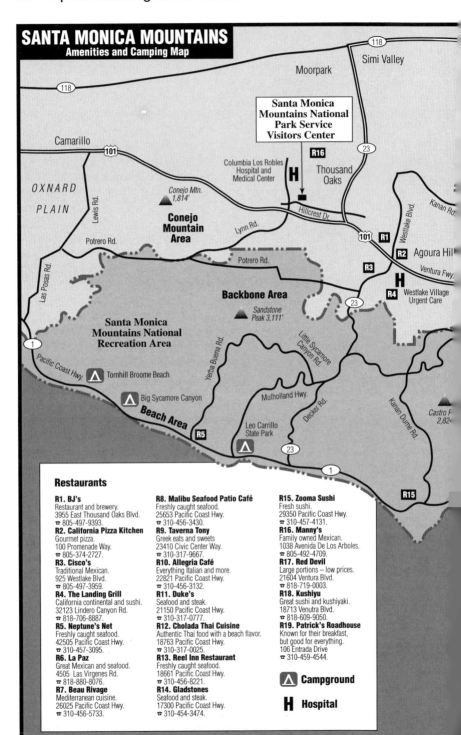

SANTA MONICA MOUNTAINS
Amenities and Camping Map

Restaurants

R1. BJ's
Restaurant and brewery.
3955 East Thousand Oaks Blvd.
☎ 805-497-9393.

R2. California Pizza Kitchen
Gourmet pizza.
100 Promenade Way.
☎ 805-374-2727.

R3. Cisco's
Traditional Mexican.
925 Westlake Blvd.
☎ 805-497-3959.

R4. The Landing Grill
California continental and sushi.
32123 Lindero Canyon Rd.
☎ 818-706-8887.

R5. Neptune's Net
Freshly caught seafood.
42505 Pacific Coast Hwy.
☎ 310-457-3095.

R6. La Paz
Great Mexican and seafood.
4505 Las Virgenes Rd.
☎ 818-880-8076.

R7. Beau Rivage
Mediterranean cuisine.
26025 Pacific Coast Hwy.
☎ 310-456-5733.

R8. Malibu Seafood Patio Café
Freshly caught seafood.
25653 Pacific Coast Hwy.
☎ 310-456-3430.

R9. Taverna Tony
Greek eats and sweets
23410 Civic Center Way.
☎ 310-317-9667.

R10. Allegria Café
Everything Italian and more.
22821 Pacific Coast Hwy.
☎ 310-456-3132.

R11. Duke's
Seafood and steak.
21150 Pacific Coast Hwy.
☎ 310-317-0777.

R12. Cholada Thai Cuisine
Authentic Thai food with a beach flavor.
18763 Pacific Coast Hwy.
☎ 310-317-0025.

R13. Reel Inn Restaurant
Freshly caught seafood.
18661 Pacific Coast Hwy.
☎ 310-456-8221.

R14. Gladstones
Seafood and steak.
17300 Pacific Coast Hwy.
☎ 310-454-3474.

R15. Zooma Sushi
Fresh sushi.
29350 Pacific Coast Hwy.
☎ 310-457-4131.

R16. Manny's
Family owned Mexican.
1038 Avenida De Los Arboles.
☎ 805-492-4709.

R17. Red Devil
Large portions – low prices.
21604 Ventura Blvd.
☎ 818-719-0003.

R18. Kushiyu
Great sushi and kushiyaki.
18713 Ventura Blvd.
☎ 818-609-9050.

R19. Patrick's Roadhouse
Known for their breakfast,
but good for everything.
106 Entrada Drive
☎ 310-459-4544.

◮ **Campground**

H Hospital

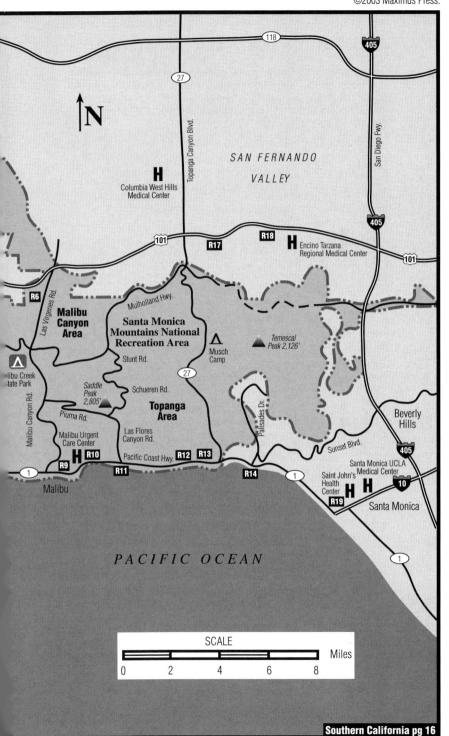

SAN FERNANDO VALLEY

H Columbia West Hills Medical Center

H Encino Tarzana Regional Medical Center

Malibu Canyon Area

Santa Monica Mountains National Recreation Area

Mulholland Hwy.

Stunt Rd.

△ Musch Camp

▲ Temescal Peak 2,126'

Saddle Peak 2,805'

Schueren Rd.

Topanga Area

Piuma Rd.

Las Flores Canyon Rd.

Malibu Urgent Care Center

Pacific Coast Hwy.

Beverly Hills

Sunset Blvd.

Palisades Dr.

Santa Monica UCLA Medical Center

Saint John's Health Center **H H**

Santa Monica

Malibu

Malibu Creek State Park

Las Virgenes Rd.

Malibu Canyon Rd.

Topanga Canyon Blvd.

San Diego Fwy.

R6, R17, R18, R10, R9, R11, R12, R13, R14, R19

PACIFIC OCEAN

SCALE

0   2   4   6   8   Miles

Southern California pg 16

Access Information

Other than the few areas mentioned specifically in their area introductions, climbing is currently allowed at all areas in this guide. This does not mean that we have carte blanche to act and do whatever we want while climbing at these areas. Several of the areas included have had access problems in the past, and discussion with the land managers regarding some of the areas is an ongoing process. Please realize the potential of your actions to impact access, act responsibly and follow these guidelines:

☞ Respect the land managers and National Park Service Rangers. Do your best to interact in a friendly manner and be sure to wave or say "hello" when you see them. Anything that can be done to keep our interactions friendly can only help in the long run.

☞ Follow the rules of each area. There are very few rules in place in the Santa Monicas. Please respect them and urge others to do the same. Only camp and park in designated areas.

☞ Stay on the established trails. One of the biggest concerns of land managers is environmental impact. Of the possible impacts, your path of travel is the most disruptive. At all areas described in this guide there are already ample trails developed to get to and from the crags. There is really no reason to create more or to try and create a shortcut.

☞ Try not to disrupt other recreational groups you come across. This is a rather broad guideline, but one that can be broken down to include radios, loud yelling and screaming, completely overtaking an area to where others won't feel welcome and other similar actions. It's always best that if any report gets back to land managers about climbers, that it be a positive one. Maintain a low profile.

☞ Don't leave trash. Whether it's yours or not—pick it up. This one action can make a huge difference. If the area you visit is overrun with trash don't get discouraged, just take it one piece at a time. Before you know it the area will be spotless and continued upkeep will be easy.

☞ If you need to "bail" from a route, leave a biner or screwlink behind instead of webbing. Not only will it be safer for the next climber on the route, it also creates a less obvious eyesore for other area users and land managers. Likewise keep chalk use to a minimum and wash or brush off all tick marks and excessive chalk when done with a route.

☞ Use toilets where provided. If there are no toilets where you're climbing dispose of your waste properly. Go at least 200 feet away from climbs, trails and water and bury any solid waste. Pack out your toilet paper in a plastic bag and try not to reuse areas in order to prevent foul odors.

☞ Volunteer for local cleanup days and other service projects and make sure that you are identified as a climber.

See Page 190

Carly Furuno on **The Ripper** 11a** at Black Flower.

First Ascent Ethics

This one section, found in just about every guidebook published, usually fuels debate. People's opinions differ and standard, accepted practices vary from area to area. The guidelines and inclusions listed below are the consensus of local route developers and have been accepted to be the preferred criteria for establishing new routes in the Santa Monica Mountains.

The Rock

First off, let's be frank. The Santa Monicas Mountains are choss! Of course there are some exceptions, but for the most part the rock at the areas described in this guide leaves something to be desired. As such, a large part of establishing new routes involves the extensive cleaning of the potential new route. There are routes found in this guide that are shining examples of what the end result of thorough cleaning can produce and there are others that saw just enough cleaning to allow for the first ascent party to succeed on the route, and nothing more. If you are considering establishing a new route in the Santa Monicas on anything less than perfect rock your first question to yourself should be whether or not you are willing to put in the time necessary to clean your proposed line. Many routes are covered with loose flakes and cobbles that must be removed. Remember that these are sport climbing areas and that the end result of your first ascent efforts should be a safe and enjoyable route. If you are not willing to put in the cleaning time that the line requires, either look for a cleaner line or don't bother establishing a route.

Chipping and Gluing

While both of these practices have been used to establish new routes at some of the areas in this guide, neither has been accepted universally within the Santa Monicas.

Chipping has many definitions; from a little heavy-handed creative cleaning with the hammer, brush or screwdriver to all out drilling of pockets with a power drill. Realize that chipping as a rule is far from accepted and is at odds with local ethics at many climbing areas. Further, one must ask himself whether or not he is robbing future climbers by creating a hold where none currently exists. Climbing standards continue to rise with every passing season and what may seem improbable or even impossible today, may match the talents of tomorrow's climbers.

Gluing has been more readily accepted at many areas in the Santa Monicas. Due to the nature of the rock, extensive cleaning of all loose rock often leaves blank, scarred and very difficult lines where originally lines of features beckoned the first ascentionist. It is not acceptable to use glue to add holds onto the rock, rather gluing is discussed as a means of reinforcing either flexing holds or key holds that are suspect for future breakage. Again the use of glue for this purpose is not entirely accepted and it is only discussed here as glue has been used widely throughout the Santa Monicas. If you choose to use glue—accept the responsibility of doing it right and doing it neatly. A good glue job will not be readily obvious upon casual inspection of the reinforced hold. If you are thinking of using glue, please consult with someone who has experience in this matter and use the proper product. Currently the best product on the market is C-100 2-part epoxy, manufactured by Hilti. Its application is made using a custom cartridge gun (also by Hilti) and requires clean, dry rock surfaces for proper adhesion. Once the glue has dried, file or sand any sharp edges and do your best to camouflage the glue to match the surrounding rock.

Anchors

Due to the soft rock found at most areas described in this guide, sleeve type bolts are the most widely used and the most preferred bolt for use in the Santa Monicas. Of these, the PowerBolt ("5-piece") by Powers-Rawl and the new Triplex bolt by Fixe are the preferred models due to their high strength ratings. As in all areas, bolts made from stainless steel are preferred over those made from mild steel for their extended life span. In extremely solid rock, and on routes less than vertical, 3/8" x 3 1/2" bolts can be used. In all other situations 1/2" x 3 1/2" bolts should be considered the minimum bolt size. Due to the soft nature of the rock a bolt is preferred and is much more reliable than a fixed piton.

Rappel bolting has been practiced at all areas described in this guide. Whether you choose to place bolts on rappel or on lead—do a good job. Think about your bolt placements and make sure that they are in the best possible locations for clipping and for insuring that the rope runs cleanly and with minimal rope drag. Make sure that you place your bolts in solid sections of rock and that they tighten down correctly. If there is any doubt as to the integrity of a placed bolt it must be removed (and the hole filled with epoxy and camouflaged) and reinstalled in a location that allows for a sound installation.

As we are discussing the establishing of sport routes, lower off anchors are a consideration as well. The minimum anchor system should be made up of chain and/or some sort of ring that would allow for the climbing rope to be passed through and the climber to rappel or be lowered off the route without having to leave anything behind. The best anchor available of this type is the Fixe Ring Anchor, and for multi-pitch climbs this is the preferred anchor system. For pitches of 30m/100' or less, an anchor made up of Fixe SuperShuts is preferred over chains or rings. These anchors are manufactured expressly for use as climbing anchors and offer a much higher strength rating than the chain and rings typically used and available at hardware or home improvement stores. They are also made of stainless steel, guaranteeing a long life span. Further, the rope can be placed into them very quickly and easily, eliminating the need for the climber to untie from his/her rope. Whatever style of anchor you choose to install make sure that it is made up of at least two points of connection to the rock and that it is installed in a location that allows for easy clipping by the climber and minimal wear on the rope.

Projects

Because of the large investment of time, energy and money involved in establishing routes in the Santa Monicas, please respect other people's projects. Projects are generally labeled in one of two ways.

A green tag on the first bolt (or first bolt of a variation to an existing route) of a route means that the route has not been climbed, but that it has been "opened" by the route's equipper to be climbed by someone else. Feel free to attempt an open project such as this.

A red tag means that a route has not been climbed and that the route's equipper is still trying the route. Due to the large amount of cleaning work that goes into establishing a route at some areas in the Santa Monicas, the route's difficulty may lie well within the equipper's abilities and the red tag signifies only that the work is not yet done on that particular route, not that the individual cannot climb the route and that you should. Please respect the equipper's wishes and stay off of the route. Remember that a limited number of individuals have chosen to donate their time, energy and money to the development of new routes and that this is done ultimately to allow you more options at the crag. Show your appreciation and gratitude of this donation by staying off of the route until it has been climbed or changed to an open project.

Another possible explanation for a red tag on a route is to warn climbers of an unsafe condition on that route. Perhaps there is a dangerously loose hold, or one of the bolts and/or anchors are loose or worn and in need of replacement. If you see a red tag on a route that you know has been redpointed already this is more than likely the reason it's there. Once the condition has been corrected the tag will be removed.

Finally, remember that just about any piece of rock can be turned into a route. Before establishing a new route, ask yourself if your proposed line will be a valid addition to the area. Further, make sure that your line does not adversely impact or encroach on surrounding routes. If, after these considerations, you decide to establish your line—**DO A GOOD JOB!**

See Page 74

Dave Hammer on **Diamond in the Rough** 11b**** at Echo Cliffs.

Climbing in the Santa Monicas

Sport climbing development in the Santa Monica Mountains has experienced a surge in recent years. Because of all of the new developments there are now many more options for climbers in the region. Not only are there new routes at the old areas, but there are also many altogether new areas. Several of the older areas in Southern California are routinely crowded on busy weekends and a climber could spend the better part of the day waiting for his turn on a given route. With all of the newer options described in this guide, climbers no longer need to deal with the crowds. Sample some of the newer areas and routes and find the peace that drew the original Santa Monica climbers to these areas.

Conduct

Our sport is made up of many different types of people, with many different attitudes and approaches to their climbing. No two individuals will bring the same thing to the crag and we will all benefit or suffer by the choices that each individual climber makes. With this in mind, please abide by the following guidelines when climbing in the Santa Monicas:

☞ If you are climbing at a crag that allows dogs, please keep an eye on your dog's actions. Most climbers will not mind an unleashed dog as long as it is well behaved and its owner is attentive to its actions. If your dog is not friendly or is not "crag trained", perhaps it would be best to leave it at home.

☞ Most climbers are drawn to climbing as an outdoor activity, where the natural surroundings, wildlife and serenity are as important as the climbing itself. Keep this in mind if you are fond of bringing a radio to the crag. If you do bring a radio and are climbing near others, ask if they would mind your listening to it at an acceptable volume. If they don't mind—thank them. If they do mind—respect their wishes and leave it off or wear headphones.

☞ On a similar note, if you are prone to screaming and/or throwing tantrums after a failed attempt, realize that your actions are affecting the experience of those around you and that they probably do not appreciate the scene.

☞ Climbing is about camaraderie and I'm sure that we've all felt the surge of adrenaline as our friends on the ground shout their encouragement. Feel free to do the same to other climbers at the crag (regardless of whether they are a part of your party or not). Likewise if you know a piece of vital beta that might help a climber on a given route, and they don't mind hearing it (ask first) give them a hand by sharing the beta.

☞ If you're waiting for a belay or see someone else that needs a belay, offer to partner up for a route. Many new partnerships have begun this way and everybody gets more climbing time in the day by eliminating unwanted "down time." Also be quick to allow others to top-rope on your route and don't hesitate to ask others if they mind your using their top-rope.

☞ Unless you are the only person that is going to be climbing a given route, clip into the anchors with quickdraws and lower off of these. This will eliminate wear on the anchors and substantially increase their life span. When the last climber is set to lower off of the route, it's very easy for him/her to clean the quickdraws and to lower directly off the anchors.

☞ After climbing a route take the time to brush off any holds that have an accumulation of chalk. This will allow the next climber on the route to get a better grip on the hold and will limit unsightly and greasy chalk buildup. This is especially necessary on extremely popular routes or after extended work sessions. Please keep in mind that most of the rock in the Santa Monicas is relatively soft. Because of this use only a nylon bristled brush. **Never** use a metal brush to clean off holds, as it will remove the texture from the hold. On a similar note, if you feel the need to mark blind holds or key "sweet spots" with a tick mark, take the time to wash it off when you're done. Many climbers do not like the visual impact that a route full of tick marks presents and onsight climbers may feel cheated by the additional information (correct or incorrect) that they offer.

☞ If you feel the need to retreat from a route before reaching the anchors please leave behind a carabiner or screwlink as opposed to a piece of webbing. This will create less of a visual impact and will insure that the next climber on the route will still be able to clip into the hanger and/or your carabiner.

☞ Some crags feature carabiners at the anchors. These have been provided for your convenience. Please realize this and do not remove them. Also, never remove quickdraws, ropes or other items off of routes or projects. These have been left intentionally and have not been abandoned. Leaving quickdraws on a project (whether it be a new route or simply an established route that a climber is trying to redpoint) is an accepted practice and the removal of these items can be viewed as nothing less than theft. If there are quickdraws on a route that you would like to attempt (and the route is not a new route project) feel free to clip into the quickdraws in place. Just remember to leave them when you are done with the route. Please note that the National Park Service has requested that no ropes be left hanging overnight.

☞ Respect any project with a red sling. The routes in the Santa Monicas have been developed by a limited number of individuals investing their own energy, money and time. Due to the nature of the rock in these areas, establishing a new route requires an immense amount of work. To steal their projects is an insult to them and their efforts to provide additional climbing options for you, and shows a severe lack of appreciation for all that these people have donated to the climbing community.

☞ Most of the areas described in this guide are approached on 100% volunteer maintained trails. Do your part to keep the trails clean and clear. Pick up all trash that you see (whether it's yours or not) and don't be afraid to carry and use a small pair of garden clippers for use on the trails. Keep your ears open for information on designated trail work days and don't hesitate to volunteer to help out.

☞ There are no bathroom facilities at most of the areas in this guide. If you need to go to the bathroom please walk far away from the climbing area and off of the trail before relieving yourself. Bury solid waste and pack out your toilet paper in a plastic bag. Try not to use the same areas that others before you have used in order to limit foul odors.

The Rock

The rock at many of the crags in this guide is a form of volcanic conglomerate known as Brecchia. There are also smaller crags of sandstone, welded tuff and even some isolated examples of conglomerate limestone. Although much of the rock found in the Santa Monica Mountains is of this same basic classification, a wide variety of features are found at the many different crags. There's something to be found for everybody's taste. From the steep cobbles of Mt. Olympus, to the immaculate limestone-like rock on some of the walls at Echo Cliffs, to the fingery pockets of Boney Bluff or the water polished pockets of Malibu Creek, to the granite like edges and flakes found at Tick Rock; very few regions can offer such a diversity of climbing in such a small geographic area.

Many of the areas described in this guide are relatively new and have yet to see the volume of traffic required to clean up all of the routes. Because of this, loose rock will still be encountered on some of the routes. Please be forewarned and prepared for this eventuality and do not stand or belay directly under climbers. If you should happen upon a loose rock while climbing, warn those on the ground below before dislodging the loose rock. If you feel that the situation warrants it, a helmet can be worn, although this should always be a personal decision.

Equipment

Almost exclusively the routes described in this guide are bolted sport routes. As such, nothing more than quickdraws and a rope are required. Bolt counts are given on all route descriptions and the few gear routes included in this guide list the type of gear required in their descriptions.

Some of the routes in this guide (most notably at Echo Cliffs) feature pitches longer than 80 feet in length. A 60 meter rope is required to lower off of, or to top-rope these routes. Please pay attention to route descriptions as they will provide a warning (30m/100') when a rope longer than 50 meters is required. It is highly suggested that a rope bag or tarp be used for flaking out your rope at the base of the routes. Many of these areas are dry and dusty and throwing your rope down in the dirt can cause tiny particles to work their way into the rope's inner core, possible damaging the nylon strands found within. Further, a dust coated rope will act as sandpaper on fixed anchors, severely decreasing their life span.

Safety Concerns

The areas described in this guide are sport climbing areas. There is a commo
misconception regarding sport climbing—that it is a completely safe endeavo
While it is safer than some other climbing pursuits it does still suffer fro
many of the same hazards and a few that seem more sport climbing relate
Use your head, as most climbing accidents are a result of poor judgment and
or a hurried approach to the act. The following climbing related accidents a
100% avoidable:

☞ Failing to tie-in properly. More and more you hear of this type of acc
dent. People get sidetracked and either forget to complete their knot or tie
to the incorrect part of their harness. Get in the habit of checking your kn
before leaving the ground. It's a good idea to recheck your knot before lowe
ing off a route as well.

☞ A similar mistake is made when the harness buckle is not doubled bac
This is usually caused by the climber being distracted and simply forgettir
to finish. It's a good idea to check your own buckle and that of your partn
before leaving the ground.

☞ With the increased popularity of sport climbing and its convenient a
proach to climbing, the use of a Gri-Gri as a belay device has become ve
common. Gri-Gris are excellent devices and once the initial adjustment peric
is over can offer a much better, safer and easier belay operation for both th
climber and the belayer. This said, there have been a fair amount of acciden
involving the rope being fed backwards through the device. When belayir
check to make sure that you have fed the rope properly and give a quick u
ward tug on the climber's end of the rope to make sure that the device
catching properly before your partner leaves the ground.

☞ While every attempt has been made to offer correct route informatic
in this guide, mistakes and / or misprints have probably occurred. Because
this whenever possible verify the correct number of bolts on a route in ord
to assure that you have enough quickdraws on your harness. Also, while a
most all of the routes in this guide have fixed anchors at the end of the rout
some of them are "closed" anchor systems where you will need an extra coup
of draws in order to attach to the system. Prepare for this when applicable b
carrying extra draws. Nothing is worse than running out of draws before reacl
ing the anchors or reaching the anchors and having nothing with which
attach to them.

☞ Many of the routes in the Santa Monicas (most notably at Echo Cliff
are long enough that they require a 60 meter rope to lower off and / or to
rope. Pay attention to the route descriptions and use a long rope where i
structed. Even on shorter routes it's a good practice to be aware of the amou
of remaining rope when lowering another climber. If there's any doubt as
whether your rope is long enough, tie a knot in the ground end of the rope
prevent it from passing through your belay device. The rock found in the San
Monicas can sometimes be loose. Be aware of this and do not belay or stan

below other climbers. If you are climbing and encounter loose rock warn anyone on the ground below you and then dislodge the rock so that it won't be a concern for future climbers. Even on popular and well-traveled routes, holds will occasionally break.

Most of the climbing areas in this guide offer at least partial cellular phone coverage either at the crag itself or at the trailhead. It is a good idea to carry your cellular phone with you in case of an accident.

Objective Hazards
There are many objective hazards to be found in the Santa Monicas. Most all of these can be found at each and every area in this guide so be prepared for any of them.

Poison Oak: The first is the scourge of Southern California rock climbing—poison oak (Toxicodendron diversilobum). Poison oak is a deciduous plant whose leaves are most commonly composed of three leaflets, where the stem of the central leaflet is longest. The leaves are notched or toothed and dark green with a paler underside. In the springtime, the plant sometimes blooms with small greenish-white flowers and in late summer can produce a whitish berry fruit. Like many deciduous trees, the leaves of poison oak change color in the fall, often turning bright red.

50% percent of the population can contract a skin irritation from coming into contact with the plant's resin or oily sap. This oil is absorbed by cells under the skin's surface producing a histaminic response as the body tries to repel the oil. Initial symptoms include irritation and itching, usually followed by small blisters and lesions. This will usually clear up within the first 10 days after contact. The plant's oil itself is the only cause of this and once the affected area is thoroughly washed, the liquid secreted by the blisters cannot spread the irritation. There are several ointments and remedies available over the counter at your local drug store that can be used to treat the irritation. In the case of a severe irritation such as swelling, consult your doctor immediately.

If you have come in contact with poison oak, wash the exposed areas of your skin with lots of cold water. As the resin is oily in nature, regular hand soap may not do a sufficient job of removing it from your skin. Isopropyl alcohol or a solution intended for the removal of oils would probably prove more effective. However, this washing should be done as soon as possible after exposure as once the oil has been absorbed by the skin, washing will not prevent an outbreak. Remember also to wash any clothing or shoes that have come in contact with poison oak as the oil remains potent long after it is rubbed off of the plant.

Rattlesnakes: Rattlesnakes can be found throughout the Santa Monicas, and can be identified primarily by the rattles on their tail, however sometimes snakes lose these. They can also be identified by their powerful body, thin neck and well-defined triangular or arrow shaped head. Their eyes are hooded and oval rather than round like nonpoisonous snakes. Especially in warm weather they will stretch across flat, exposed areas in order to soak up the heat of the sun. When not sunning, rattlesnakes can usually be found in areas of dense brush or jumbled, rocky areas.

It is a common belief that rattlesnakes are aggressive. This is entirely untrue. In most cases they will only attack if they feel threatened and have no options for escape. The actual act of "rattling" is meant to alert you to their presence and to offer a warning. If you hear this rattling, stop what you are doing and move away from the sound. Unless you have no escape route yourself, do not poke at the snake with a stick or throw rocks at it as this will only put the snake in a more defensive position where an attack is more likely.

Although you hear of several rattlesnake sightings, it is extremely uncommon to hear of bites. And less than 1/2% of those bitten die as a result of their bite. In fact, up to 60% of snake bites are what is known as a "dry bite," where no venom is released by the snake. If you watch your step and steer clear of snakes if and when you see them, you should have no problems with them whatsoever. Always give snakes the right of way.

What **to do** in case of a bite:

☞ Move away from the snake in order to prevent further bites.

☞ Remain calm and place the bitten limb in a comfortable position at a level slightly lower than the victim's heart.

☞ Look for the exact site of the bite (you should be able to see the fang punctures).

☞ If you have a Sawyer Pump Extractor®, or other suitable venom extractor (available at most larger sporting goods or hunting stores for about $10.00) select a cup size that covers both punctures and begin use (it's a good idea to read the instructions ahead of time).

☞ If you do not have a venom extractor, apply hard pressure to the puncture area with a clean cloth and tape in place with climbing or other adhesive tape.

☞ In either of the above first aid treatments, you should now wrap a

ACE bandage or wide cloth strip around the bitten limb just above the puncture site. Wrap with approximately the same tightness that you would for a sprained ankle, but not too tightly. Check periodically for a pulse below your wrap to make sure that it is not too tight. If you are ever unable to find a pulse rewrap the bandage looser.

☞ Get to a hospital as soon as possible. Most available information suggests a time of one to one and a half hours from the time of the bite as being an acceptable time frame for best treatment options. Call ahead, if possible, and let them know that you are on the way, or that you need assistance. Have them make sure that they have antivenin on hand.

☞ Call the California Poison Control System anytime, anyplace in California at 1-800-876-4766.

What **not to do** in case of a bite:
- ☞ **Don't** apply a tourniquet.
- ☞ **Don't** apply ice or heat to the puncture site.
- ☞ **Don't** cut the puncture site.
- ☞ **Don't** use your mouth to suck out the venom.
- ☞ **Don't** give the victim drugs or alcohol.
- ☞ **Don't** apply electric shock.
- ☞ **Don't** remove the venom extractor or dressings until you are instructed to do so by a medical attendant.
- ☞ **Don't** attempt to capture or kill the snake. In all modern medical facilities the same antivenin is used.

Ticks: Ticks are small (roughly 1/3") arthropods that feed on the blood of larger mammals, and are usually found on long grasses and bushes at the edge of small wooded areas. They crawl up onto the grasses and bushes and cling to you as you brush up against the plant while walking by. If you find yourself walking through an area such as this check yourself frequently for ticks and brush them off if you find any. Wearing lighter colored clothing can make it much easier to see the ticks as they are usually dark brown or black in color.

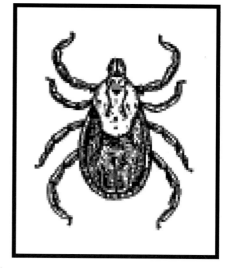

Ticks are carriers of several diseases that can affect humans including Rocky Mountain Spotted Fever and Lyme Disease. Both of these are rare and highly treatable with an early detection. If you do not find a tick right away and it has the opportunity to attach itself to your skin, do not worry as it usually relatively easy to remove a tick. The easiest way to do this is to grasp the tick as close as possible to your skin with a pair of tweezers. Pull the tick straight out from your skin slowly and firmly. The tick will usually release its hold and come out with no problems whatsoever. Don't use any of the folklore methods for removing a tick (cigarettes, gasoline or matches) as these will only irritate the tick and cause it to regurgitate into your skin, increasing the likelihood that a disease will be transmitted. Likewise covering the tick in oil or butter will not work as the breathing orifices on a tick are so small that it can survive for hours while covered in oil. After removing the tick wash the area with alcohol or a medical antiseptic and keep an eye on it for the next few days. If you are unable to remove all of the tick (if you pull too quickly the head can sometimes break off inside your skin) or if a rash develops around the area, consult your doctor immediately.

Sun Exposure: Especially when climbing during the summer months, you can be exposed to direct sunlight and high temperatures for an extended period of time. Because of this it is a good idea to use a sufficiently strong enough sunscreen to prevent sunburn. Wear a hat and long sleeve shirts if you are particularly susceptible to sunburn and try to follow the shade that is available at most areas in this guide.

With the heat comes the need to drink plenty of fluids. Make sure to bring enough water with you to the crag and stay well hydrated throughout the day. At the end of the day be sure to replenish you body with electrolyte drinks and/or additional water. Use the old urine test: if your urine is yellow you need more fluids, if it's clear you're doing just fine.

In Case of Accident:

It is a good idea to carry and know how to use a basic first aid kit. They don't take up much room in your pack and even a simple kit can address most basic injuries. If you use something from your kit make sure to restock it so that it, and you, are always ready for whatever might occur.

Most cell phones have at least partial coverage of the Santa Monica Mountains. Because of this you should pack yours in the event that assistance is needed or to alert a medical provider that you are heading their way.

Should you need medical attention beyond your abilities, medical care is available at any of the following locations (map page 20):

• **Columbia Los Robles Hospital and Medical Center**
215 West Janss Road
Thousand Oaks, CA 91360
☎ 805-497-2727
Available 24 hours every day.

• **Westlake Village Urgent Care**
4415 South Lakeview Canyon Road
Westlake Village, CA 91361
☎ 818-874-0900
Available from 7:00 A.M. until 7:00 P.M. every day.

• **Columbia West Hills Medical Center**
7300 Medical Center Drive
West Hills, CA 91307
☎ 818-676-4000
Available 24 hours every day.

• **Encino Tarzana Regional Medical Center**
16237 Ventura Blvd.
Encino, CA 91436
☎ 818-995-5000
Available 24 hours every day.

• **Saint John's Health Center**
1328 Twenty-Second Street
Santa Monica, CA 90404
☎ 310-829-5511
Available 24 hours every day.

• **Santa Monica UCLA Medical Center**
1250 Sixteenth Street
Santa Monica, CA 90404
☎ 310-319-4000
Available 24 hours every day.

• **Malibu Urgent Care Center**
23656 Pacific Coast Highway
Malibu, CA 90265
☎ 310-456-7551
Available Monday through Friday from 10:00 A.M. until 7:00 P.M.
Saturday and Sunday from 10:00 A.M. until 6:00 P.M.

How to Use This Guide

The Santa Monica Mountains parallel the Pacific Ocean stretching from the City of Los Angeles northward to the Camarillo Basin. The climbing areas located in the Santa Monicas are spread throughout a fairly large area, and their description in this guide has been broken into five separate area chapters. Specific information pertaining to each area is covered in that chapter, however conditions at most included crags are similar and the general information supplied in this introduction should be treated as applicable to all areas.

Maps

This book features a number of exploding maps. The first is an Overview Map (page 40) which shows the general layout of the Santa Monica Mountains and the individual areas. The Area Maps will help you find the individual crags and assist you in driving to them. Approach Maps show the final driving directions as well as the hike to the crags. After this more complex crags may have Crag Maps and Cliff Overviews. The page numbers listed with the maps will allow you to zoom in and out as necessary

Approach Instructions

The approach instructions will be found at the beginning of each individual crag's introduction. Referencing the Area Map (at the beginning of each chapter) and the Approach Map should get you where your going.

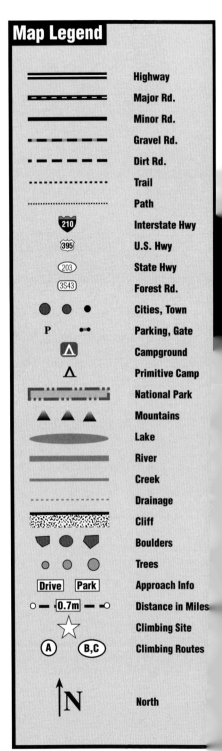

Difficulty Ratings

Pitches have been rated according to the Yosemite Decimal System. The 5th class prefix has been dropped for simplicity. Every effort has been made to eliminate "slash" ratings (i.e.: a/b, b/c, c/d). However, some slash ratings will still be found in this guide. These ratings generally represent one of two things. Either a route is new enough or there is not sufficient information on the route to establish a comfortable consensus as to that route's difficulty, or it may involve a reachy or otherwise height dependent move that would affect the rating of the climb.

Boulder problems have been rated using the V-scale. This is the most widely accepted bouldering scale. Some problems will also have a notation of (highball) or (h) shown with the difficulty rating. This would suggest that either the difficult moves are found near the top of a tall problem or that the boulder is quite tall. In either case extra caution should be taken on problems that have been notated highballs.

Ratings	
YDS	Verm
5.9	VB
10a	V0-
10b	V0-
10c	V0
10d	V0+
11a	V1
11b	V2
11c	V2
11d	V3
12a	V4
12b	V5
12c	V6
12d	V6
13a	V7
13b	V8
13c	V9
13d	V10
14a	V11
14b	V11
14c	V12
14d	V13

Quality Ratings

Quality ratings have been assigned based on the following factors: the amount of sustained climbing, the aesthetics of the moves, pump factor, exposure, location and rock quality. Squeeze Jobs, contrived lines and poorly equipped routes subtract from the quality rating.

*****	Area Classic
****	Awesome
***	Excellent
**	Good
*	Worth Doing
no stars	Poor

Following the quality rating an (r) indicates a runout route, an (x) indicates a very dangerous route, and an (h) indicates a highball boulder problem.

Route Descriptions

Following the name of the route and its difficulty and quality ratings, is a description of the gear that is required. First listed is the number of bolts found on the route, followed by any gear that might be required. Pitches longer than 25 meters/80 feet are then noted (30m/100'). Be sure to pay attention and use a 60-meter rope on these pitches. Next is a brief description of the route. Finally listed is the first ascent information. FA signifies the person or persons involved in the first redpoint of the route. Generally the first name listed is the individual who made the first redpoint. OB signifies that the route has not yet been redpointed, but that the individual moves have been climbed by the person listed. EB signifies that the person listed equipped the route with its hardware, but at present that is all that has happened with the route. FTR signifies the first person to top-rope the route.

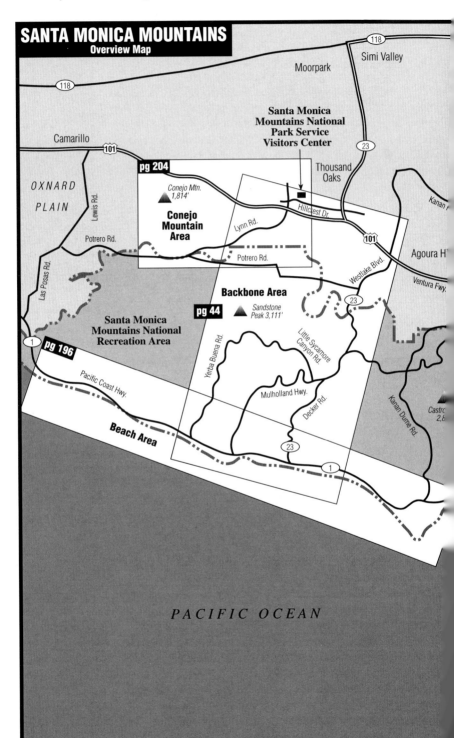

SANTA MONICA MOUNTAINS
Overview Map

118

Simi Valley

Moorpark

Santa Monica
Mountains National
Park Service
Visitors Center

Camarillo

101

23

Thousand
Oaks

OXNARD

PLAIN

Lewis Rd.

pg 204

Conejo Mtn.
1,814'

Conejo
Mountain
Area

Lynn Rd.

Hillcrest Dr.

Kanan r

Potrero Rd.

Las Posas Rd.

Potrero Rd.

Potrero Rd.

101

Westlake Blvd.

Agoura H

Ventura Fwy.

Backbone Area

23

pg 44

Sandstone
Peak 3,111'

Santa Monica
Mountains National
Recreation Area

1

pg 196

Pacific Coast Hwy.

Yerba Buena Rd.

Little Sycamore
Canyon Rd.

Mulholland Hwy.

Decker Rd.

Kanan Dume Rd.

Castro
2,8

Beach Area

23

1

PACIFIC OCEAN

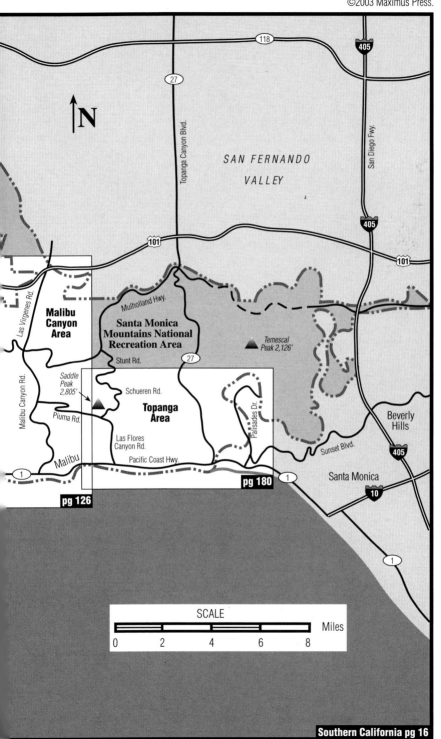

N

118

27

405

405

San Diego Fwy.

SAN FERNANDO

VALLEY

Topanga Canyon Blvd.

101

101

Las Virgenes Rd.

Mulholland Hwy.

**Malibu
Canyon
Area**

**Santa Monica
Mountains National
Recreation Area**

Temescal
Peak 2,126'

Stunt Rd.

27

Saddle
Peak
2,805'

Schueren Rd.

**Topanga
Area**

Malibu Canyon Rd.

Piuma Rd.

Palisades Dr.

Beverly
Hills

Las Flores
Canyon Rd.

Malibu

Pacific Coast Hwy.

Sunset Blvd.

405

1

pg 180

1

Santa Monica

10

pg 126

1

SCALE

Miles

0   2   4   6   8

See Page 60

Louie Anderson on **Power of One** 13d***** at Echo Cliffs. ©*Perri Nguyen Photo.*

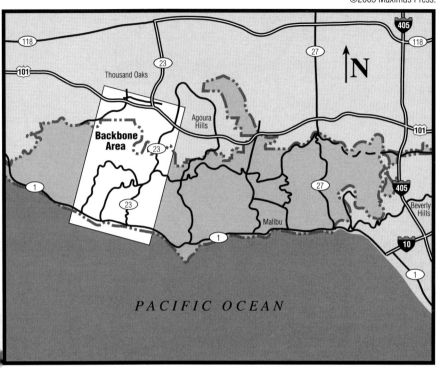

CHAPTER 2

BACKBONE AREA

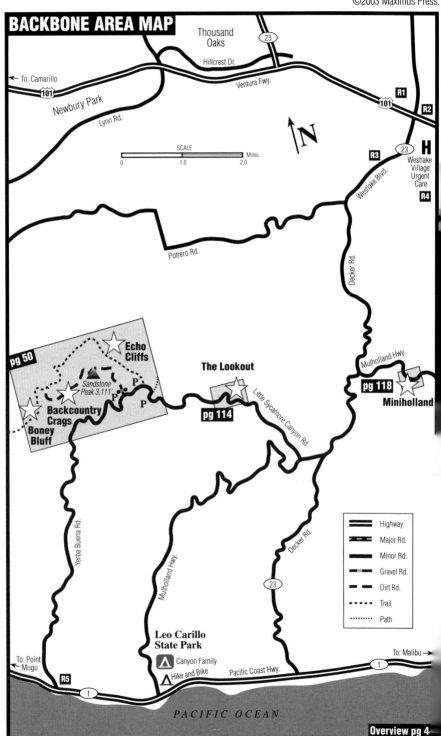

BACKBONE AREA MAP

Thousand Oaks

23

Hillcrest Dr.

To: Camarillo ←

Ventura Fwy.

101

R1

101

R2

Newbury Park

Lynn Rd.

N

R3   23   H

Westlake Village Urgent Care

R4

SCALE

0   1.0   2.0   Miles

Westlake Blvd.

Potrero Rd.

Decker Rd.

pg 50

Echo Cliffs

The Lookout

Mulholland Hwy.

Sandstone Peak 3,111'

P

P

P

Little Sycamore Canyon Rd.

pg 118

Miniholland

pg 114

Backcountry Crags

Boney Bluff

P

Yerba Buena Rd.

Mulholland Hwy.

Decker Rd.

23

	Highway
	Major Rd.
	Minor Rd.
	Gravel Rd.
	Dirt Rd.
	Trail
	Path

Leo Carillo State Park

Canyon Family

Hike and Bike

To: Malibu →

To: Point Mugu ←

R5

1

Pacific Coast Hwy.

1

PACIFIC OCEAN

Overview pg 4

BACKBONE AREA BASICS

T he Backbone Area encompasses the future of Santa Monica Mountains climbing. The sheer quantity of rock in this area is staggering. Echo Cliffs is the area's premier attraction, however the difficult, power-based routes found at Boney Bluff offer a style of climbing found nowhere else in Southern California. Recent developments in the backcountry have resulted in a collection of smaller crags that have proven quite popular, and as the fingers of development probe further, rest assured that many new areas will be discovered and developed for climbing.

Getting There

Most of the crags located in the Backbone Area are approached from one of two trailheads. These are the Backbone / Sandstone Peak Trailhead and the Mishe Mokwa Trailhead. Both trailheads can be reached from either the Ventura Fwy. (101) or the Pacific Coast Hwy. (1).

Restaurants

R1. BJ's
Restaurant and brewery.
3955 E. Thousand Oaks Blvd.
☎ 805-497-9393.

R2. California Pizza Kitchen
Gourmet pizza.
100 Promenade Way.
☎ 805-374-2727.

R3. Cisco's
Traditional Mexican.
925 Westlake Blvd.
☎ 805-497-3959.

R4. The Landing Grill
California continental and sushi.
32123 Lindero Canyon Rd.
☎ 818-706-8887.

R5. Neptune's Net
Freshly caught seafood.
42505 Pacific Coast Hwy.
☎ 310-457-3095.

Camping

Leo Carrillo State Park
Canyon Family
Open all year, the fee is $12. Picnic tables, piped water, showers, flush toilets, pets OK, elev. sea level.
☎ 800-444-7275.

Hike and Bike (walk-in)
Open all year, the fee is $1. Picnic tables, piped water, showers, flush toilets, pets OK, elev. sea level.
☎ 805-488-5223.

Nicole on **Superfly** 10a**** at Echo Cliffs.

See Page 55

See Page 79   Dan Portman on **Gravity** 11d****. ©*Perri Nguyen Photo.*

Echo Cliffs

Echo Cliffs is fast becoming the premier sport climbing venue for Los Angeles and Ventura based climbers. The number of climbers at the cliff has risen steadily in the last few seasons, and the increased traffic on the routes has cleaned off the final bit of loose rock. Unlike other popular Southern California sport climbing areas, the popular routes at Echo are not limited to one or two individual walls. Because of this the crowding and lines, found elsewhere, have not yet become a problem here.

Echo Cliffs Details

Elevation: 2,200 ft.
Exposure: Varied, sun and shade.
Sport Climbs: 152 routes, 5.5 to 14a/b.
Drive From Hwy 101: 20 minutes.
Drive From Hwy 1: 15 minutes.
Approach: 25 to 55 minute hike.

With over 150 routes to choose from, climbers can enjoy a wide variety of climbing styles, route lengths and wall steepness. The multidirectional quality of the cliffline also ensures that either sunshine or shade can be found at any time of the day, depending on your preference.

Many of the routes found at Echo are long; and some require a 60-meter rope to lower off or to top-rope the route. Because of this it's a good idea to always climb with a 60-meter rope. If you are climbing with a shorter rope please pay special attention to the route descriptions, as they will warn when a 60-meter rope is required (30m/100′). All routes are bolt-protected and have fixed anchors at their end.

History: The climbing history at Echo Cliffs, and other areas of the Santa Monica Mountains, all began with one name—Jeff Willis. Willis was an avid trail runner and when local brush fires in the early 1990s cleared the hillsides and made several areas accessible, he began systematically running sections of the Santa Monicas in a search for climbable rock. Before long he had discovered a handful of separate areas that he felt had distinct potential for sport climbing.

While it wasn't the first area that Willis discovered, Echo was by far the best. The White Wall in particular had caught Willis' eye and while its lines were more difficult than his climbing abilities at that time, he immediately placed a few directional bolts and began attempting what was later to became *State of Grace*.

Willis began carrying photos of the area with him and showing them to individuals that he felt might be interested in helping to develop the areas he had found. Southern California at that time had a small group of new route activists and many of them saw these photos and either responded or chose to wait and see what became of the area. Some of the first to go out with him were Louie Anderson, Steve Edwards and Jack Marshall. Anderson and Marshall in particular took an interest in Echo and on a day early in the development of the crag the obvious lines and walls were split up among the group. In fact, the first completed route at the crag was a joint bolting effort between Anderson and Willis called *The Daily Grind*.

Anderson was initially most interested in the Java Wall and the Zombie Wall. Marshall focused mainly on the Pink Wall and showed interest in a cave at the far right of the crag that later became home to some of the most popular steep routes at Echo. Many of the better routes at Echo were climbed during this initial wave including *Java, Split Decision, Restrain This* and *Thunderkiss*.

Everyone involved was having fun and enjoying the new climbing options that Echo provided when it all came to an end. A portion of the crag lies on National Park Service (NPS) land and the local rangers began to notice an increase in the number of cars at the Mishe Mokwa trailhead. They investigated what was going on at Echo and surprisingly did not have any immediate concerns with the bolting being performed there. However, they did have concerns over the trail that was being used to access the cliff. Unbeknownst to those who forged this initial trail, it cut right through a patch of endangered plant life that was only found in this portion of the Santa Monicas. This being their primary concern, but also worrying about possible impact to other plant and animal life of the area, the cliff was closed to climbing while an impact study could be performed. During the closure a handful of local climbers and the Access Fund joined forces to open discussions with the NPS. The local ranger in charge at that time wanted to see the area reopened to climbers and was very instrumental in the tone of the ensuing negotiations. A new access trail was planned and approved by the NPS, and on a happy day roughly a year after the closure a team of volunteers, made up primarily of local climbers, worked together to build the trail which now leaves the Split Rock Picnic Area to approach the crag.

With the blessing of the NPS, development began again in earnest. Anderson wrapped up the remaining routes on the Java Wall including the classic *Caffeine*. He also moved on to other walls, adding *The Stain* and *Meager and Weak*. Chris Murray and local Eric Hinds also became involved during this period and worked together to create the always popular arete of *Bushed Coyote*.

Now that the initial obvious lines had been climbed, activists began looking at other walls for potential. Perhaps the most visionary in this sense was Marshall who went on to install top anchors and random bolts on several faces. Unfortunately for Echo, Marshall discovered another climbing area around this time and refocused his energy and drive on the development of that area. Nevertheless, the focussed inspection of the other walls at Echo by Marshall and Anderson showed the area to have far more potential than first imagined. Around the same time Willis was given an excellent business opportunity with a new start up company and left the development of Echo altogether.

During the following years Anderson teamed up with whoever was willing and continued to bolt lines along the length of the cliff. Highlights from this period include *Espresso, The Power of One, Carnivore, Kamikaze, Crash and Burn* and *Prodigy*. After climbing these, and realizing that Marshall and Willis would not be returning, Anderson began focussing on their abandoned projects. These lines were among the best at Echo and resulted in routes like *State of Grace, Buried Treasure, No Remorse* and *Hijacked*. Around this time the classic *Immaculate* was climbed as well.

Echo's popularity was on the rise, and with the influx of new climbers came new vision. Doniel Drazin realized the further potential of Echo among his first visits to the crag. Drazin and Anderson began climbing together and the pace of development at the crag increased. Drazin saw lines where none had previously looked. Perhaps the best examples of this vision are the routes *Calm* and *Cloud Nine*. Both of these routes were immediately popular and were smack dab in the middle of some of the first areas developed.

Anderson and Drazin began looking at the taller faces at the right end of Echo and bolted several popular routes. The joint effort of *Blackjack* showed the potential for multi-pitch routes and Drazin's *Casey at the Bat* is a long pitch that is one of the best 5.10's at the crag. Drazin also succeeded on his classic *Devotion* during this period.

Recent developments show no signs of slowing down. Entire new areas like The Shrine, the Tower of Zen, the Test Site and the Energy Wall, as well as recent developments at the Treasure Towers show that Echo is far from being climbed out. Some of the routes at these areas like *Buddha Belly, Shiva, Meditation Station, Chi, Spontaneous Wisdom, Windfall, Diamond in the Rough* and *Booty* are classics for their grade.

In early 2002, NPS rangers once again became interested in the increased number of climbers and hikers on the Mishe Mokwa trail and at the cliff. They realized that the popularity of the area had increased and approached local climbers again with impact concerns. As before, an open dialogue began between the NPS and the climbing community. Just before the release of this guide, the NPS met with archaeologists and botanists at the crag and were able to clear the area of any possibility of archaeological sites and found no adverse impacts as a result of climber use. Members of both the NPS and the climbing community performed minimal clean up duties at the crag and took steps to better identify primary trail patterns at the cliff. Erosion impacts were addressed and plans for future signage and toilet facilities at the trailhead were made. The NPS also approved a new approach trail down the main drainage opposite the Java Wall. The use of this approach reduces the hiking time to the crag by roughly 15 minutes. This open communication and willing cooperation on both sides is a refreshing example of the possible relationship between climbers and land managers, and should allow for continued enjoyment of the area by all interested recreational groups.

Adapted from the U.S.G.S 1:24,000 Triunfo Pass and Newbury Park Quadrangles.

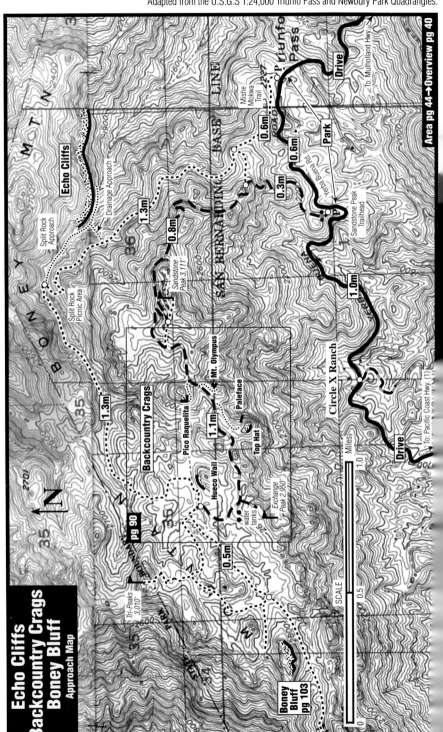

Echo Cliffs
Backcountry Crags
Boney Bluff
Approach Map

The Approach: *Ventura Freeway (101):* Exit the freeway at the Westlake Blvd. (23) exit and head south (towards the ocean). You will pass through a couple of traffic signals before coming to a stop sign at Potrero Rd. (mile 1.6 from the 101). Continue through this stop sign, passing a large rock formation on your right until you reach another stop sign at Carlisle Canyon Rd. (mile 2.7). Drive straight through this intersection and follow the road as it winds up through the hills. At mile 4.7 you will merge with Mulholland Dr., which comes in from your left. Continue on through this intersection until you reach a stop sign (mile 6.4), with Mulholland Dr. continuing on your right. Turn here and then turn right again onto Little Sycamore Canyon Rd. (mile 6.7). This road will wind through the hills, changing name to Yerba Buena Rd. and passing a small development of homes at a sharp left turn in the road (mile 8.5) before reaching the Mishe Mokwa Trailhead at mile 10.3. Parking is found in the turnouts on either side of the road and the trail starts directly from the right hand turnout.

Pacific Coast Highway (1): From the Pacific Coast Hwy., head inland on Yerba Buena Rd. (located adjacent to Neptune's Net restaurant). Head up into the hills, passing a junction with Cortharin Rd. after 2.9 miles. At 3.8 miles you will pass the Circle X Ranger Station on your right and then the Backbone Trailhead at mile 4.8. Continue on to mile 5.4. This is the Mishe Mokwa trailhead. Parking is found in the turnouts on either side of the road and the trail starts directly from the left hand turnout.

Decker Road (23): You can also leave the Pacific Coast Hwy. (1) and head inland on Decker Rd. (23 North). Follow this road for 4.8 miles until you reach a stop sign at Mulholland Dr., which comes in from your left. Turn left here and continue to a right turn onto Little Sycamore Canyon Rd. (mile 5.1 from the Pacific Coast Hwy.). This road will wind through the hills, changing names to Yerba Buena Rd. and passes a small development of homes at a sharp left turn in the road (mile 6.9) before reaching the Mishe Mokwa trailhead at mile 8.7. Parking is found in the turnouts on either side of the road and the trail starts directly from the right hand turnout.

From the Mishe Mokwa Trailhead, follow the trail uphill. At approximately .6 miles you will reach a junction with the Backbone connector trail, which cuts back uphill on your left. Continue on the Mishe Mokwa trail as it drops into and skirts the valley below. Once you are facing the cliffline itself, you will pass a large flat rock, immediately off the right side of the trail, with the word "ECHO" spray painted on it. If this is your first time to the area this is a good place to stop and get a feel for where the different walls lie on the cliff. About 5 minutes after passing this rock a wide, smooth downhill section of trail will end at a gully before heading back uphill. This is the junction with the Drainage Approach. This is the preferred and most direct approach to the crag. Head downhill following the rock bottomed gully until it ends at a large rock. Scramble down this rock on your left and follow the trail until it ends at the Grotto Area. Approximately 25-40 minutes hiking time.

Another approach option is to continue past the Drainage Approach junc-

Echo Cliffs

Balanced Rock

The Far Side page 80

Wasteland page 72

Dihedrals page 54

Approach Map page 50

tion to Split Rock Picnic Area. About 100 feet after passing through the picnic area, a faint trail leaves the main trail on your right. This is the original climber's trail. Follow it as it parallels the creekbed and traverses the left side of the canyon, heading back to the crag. A short while after coming up out of the initial creek area you will reach a rocky section where the trail seems to head uphill. Instead of heading uphill here, cross over the top of the rocks and drop down to the continuation of the climber's trail. From this point on, the trail is very easy to follow. Once you reach the beginning of the cliffline, head down into the creekbed (on your right) and follow the creekbed until you reach the Grotto Area. Approximately 40-55 minutes hiking time.

Balanced Rock

Echo Cliffs Intro: Page 47. Balanced Rock is the obvious landmark spire located on the hillside above the main clifline. Despite its appearance to the contrary, it's not going anywhere. There are currently two routes on the spire. They are in the shade in the afternoon.

Heirloom 9(r)
Climbs the old bolt ladder. No one knows the origin of the bolt ladder, but the route was free climbed to reach the summit in order to equip the next route.
FA: Kevin Daniels, 1996.

Get the Balance Right 11c*
6 bolts to a 2 bolt anchor on the summit. This route climbs the center of the steep side of the spire passing several large huecos.
FA: Reese Martin, Craig Pearson, 1997.

See Page 83 Jean Delataillade catches the pocket on **No Remorse** 13b*****. ©Ryan Wedemeyer Photo.

Echo Cliffs Photo page 52

Test Site page 70

Zombie Wall page 69

Pink Wall page 66

Chocolate Wall page 62

White Wall page 60

Java Wall page 58

Left Flank page 57

Wasteland page 72

Grotto

Dihedrals
A. Welcome to Echo 10a**
B. Bushed Coyote 10d***
C. Morning Glory 9*
D. Java 11d*****
E. Power of One 13d*****
F. Calm 12a****
G. Restrain This 11b****
H. Thunderkiss 12d***

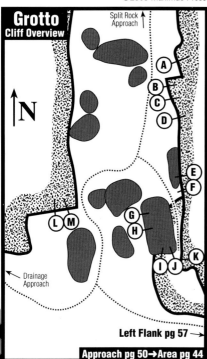

Grotto
Cliff Overview

Split Rock
Approach ↑

N

Drainage
Approach

Left Flank pg 57 →

Approach pg 50→Area pg 44

Grotto

Echo Cliffs Intro: Page 47. A very popular area located in the creekbed below the main cliffline. The Grotto is a great place to climb on a hot day as you can escape the heat by climbing under the canopy of the huge Sycamore trees. There is usually water here during the springtime. Thanks to the trees the routes here enjoy mixed shade all day long.

A. Xanadu 7**
bolts to 2 open shuts. Climb black slab passing a small roof and a thin pocket crux.
FA: Louie Anderson, 2001.

B. Intensity 11b***
bolts to shared 3 open shuts. After clipping first bolt, move left to the arete and climb over the bulge using hard to see pockets. Action packed for its size.
FA: Louie Anderson, 1998.

C. Slammer 10b*
3 bolts to shared 3 open shuts. After clipping first bolt, traverse right and climb up the right arete using large holds on the left face.
FA: Louie Anderson, 1998.

D. Lowrider 10b**
3 bolts to 2 open shuts. Climb through a bouldery crux to the large ledge above.
FA: Louie Anderson, 1998.

E. Superfly 10a****
5 bolts to 2 open shuts. Stick clip first bolt or commit to the starting moves. Climb straight up past amazingly large features for the angle. ➤ Photo page 45.
FA: Louie Anderson, 1998.

F. Air Ranger 10c**
7 bolts to double biners. Climb the face to the right of *Superfly* and then up the blunt arete above.
FA: Louie Anderson, 1998.

G. Dipstick 12b***
7 bolts to 2 open shuts. Start in the pit below and climb up tensiony 5.11 moves on sidepulls and underclings to a rest at the horizontal break. After lingering here, punch through the powerful headwall crux.
FA: Louie Anderson, 1998.

H. Nimrod 10d***
5 bolts to 2 open shuts. Climb the low angle face to a good rest at a horizontal break, then continue up the steeper headwall above.
FA: Louie Anderson 1998.

I. Junior 9*
3 bolts to shared 2 open shuts. Cautiously climb to the first bolt (these are the hardest moves on the route) and then up and right to a shared anchor.
FA: Louie Anderson, 1998.

J. Little Giant 8*
3 bolts to shared 2 open shuts. Climb the right arete.
FA: Louie Anderson, 1998.

K. Stubby 12a
2 bolts to 2 open shuts. After stick clipping first bolt, climb through a bouldery crux.
FA: Louie Anderson, 1998.

L. Miss Pacman 9***
5 bolts to shared 2 open shuts. Climb straight up the slightly less than vertical face on balancey, technical moves.
FA: Doniel Drazin, 2001.

M. Game Boy 8**
6 bolts to shared 2 open shuts. Climb the arete and then go left at the top to the anchors.
FA: Louie Anderson, 1998.

See Page 59

Chris Murray reaches for a sloping edge on **Espresso** 11a*****.

Jean Delataillade on **Bushed Coyote** 10d***.

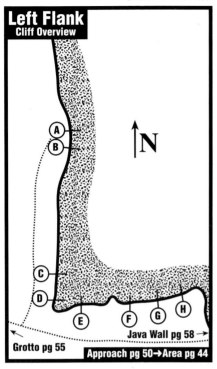

Left Flank

Echo Cliffs Intro: Page 47. The Left Flank is the farthest left end of the main cliffline. All routes left of the Java Wall are included in this area. There is still quite a bit of potential here for shorter, moderate routes on the tier directly above the Grotto. The routes of the Left Flank are only in the shade in the morning, with the exception of the large slab left of the Java Wall which goes back into the shade in the late afternoon.

A. Welcome to Echo 10a**
5 bolts to chain anchors. Climb up the left face passing interesting pockets around the edge to a final steep bulge.
FA: Louie Anderson, 1997.

B. Reverb 10a
5 bolts to chain anchor. Climb up the groove on somewhat loose rock.
FA: Louie Anderson, 1997.

C. Open project
The line left of *Bushed Coyote*, with only the anchors installed.

D. Bushed Coyote 10d***
5 bolts to 2 open shuts. Climbs the arete, finishing in the hand crack above. A very popular route.
➤ Photo this page.
FA: Chris Murray, 1996.

E. Wet Bush 10b**
6 bolts to 2 open shuts. Climbs the thin face over a small roof.
FA: Chris Murray, 1997.

F. Morning Glory 9*
6 bolts to 2 open shuts. One of the original routes at Echo. Climb up the left side of the slab, passing well-spaced bolts.
FA: Chris Murray, 1995.

G. Bushwacked 9*
9 bolts to 2 open shuts, 30m/100'. Bolted as part of Doniel's Birthday Challenge in 2000. Climb the steep, center of the slab.
FA: Doniel Drazin, 2000.

H. B-line 10a*
8 bolts to 2 open shuts, 30m/100'. Also a product of the 2000 Birthday Challenge. The route at the far right of the slab.
FA: Doniel Drazin, 2000.

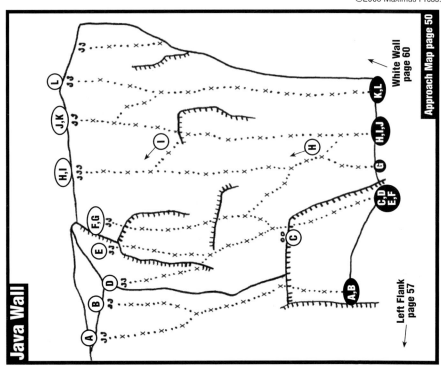

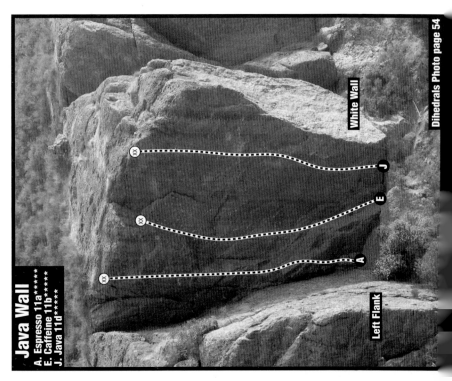

Java Wall

A. Espresso 11a*****
E. Caffeine 11b*****
J. Java 11d******

Java Wall

Echo Cliffs Intro: Page 47. Perhaps the most visible wall at Echo when approaching from the Mishe Mokwa trail, the Java Wall lies directly opposite the Drainage approach. This wall features some of the best long moderate routes at the crag and all of the routes found here are primarily stamina challenges. The Java Wall routes are in the shade in the morning.

A. Espresso 11a★★★★★
12 bolts to 2 open shuts, 30m/100'. Start at the far left of the face. Climb a short, steep starting block to an easy slab section. From here continue up the arete and traverse left, following the left bolt line to the top of the wall. One of the most popular "warm-ups" at the crag. ➤ Photo page 56.
FA: Louie Anderson, 1998.

B. Cappuccino 11c★★★★★
12 bolts to 2 open shuts, 30m/100'. Start as for *Espresso*, but after clipping its 8th bolt climb straight up the right bolt line past powerful pocket moves.
FA: Doniel Drazin, 2001.

C. Ramp Route 5
3 bolts to 2 ring anchors. Climb the low angle ramp to the ledge above.
FA: Louie Anderson, 1996.

D. Kona 13b★★
12 bolts to 2 open shuts, 30m/100'. Begin on *Caffeine*, but after clipping its 8th bolt climb left onto the steep face. Continue up this passing a pair of slopey ledge jugs to small holds and long moves.
FA: Louie Anderson, 1997.

E. Caffeine 11b★★★★★
12 bolts to 2 open shuts, 30m/100'. Climb *Ramp Route* and then continue past its anchors, climbing diagonally up and left toward the obvious dihedral above. Continue up this dihedral and the face to its right to a final steep flake section. Amazing!
FA: Louie Anderson, 1996.

F. Americano 11a★★★
11 bolts to 2 open shuts, 30m/100'. Start as for *Caffeine*, but after clipping its 4th bolt climb slightly to the right and then straight up, passing over a roof and several huge pockets to the ledge above.
FA: Louie Anderson, 1996.

G. French Roast 12a★★★
13 bolts to 2 open shuts, 30m/100'. Start just to the right of *Ramp Route* and climb straight up on easy moves to the 3rd bolt of *Death Before Decaf*. From here climb up and left and after clipping its 5th bolt continue left to join and finish on *Americano*. An alternate start (better quality and difficulty) is to start on *Java* and then cut left following *Death Before Decaf*.
FA: Louie Anderson, 1994.

H. Death Before Decaf 12a★★★
13 bolts to 3 open shuts, 30m/100'. Start as for *Java*, but after clipping its 2nd bolt climb up and left clipping 3 more bolts before climbing up and slightly right past an underling and some small edges. From here fight the pump and make a beeline for the top of the wall.
FA: Louie Anderson, 1995.

I. Sumatra 11d★★★
12 bolts to 3 open shuts, 30m/100'. A link-up. Start on *Java* and climb to its 8th bolt. After clipping this, climb left passing 1 independent bolt before finishing on *Death Before Decaf*.
FA: Louie Anderson, 1995.

J. Java 11d★★★★★
12 bolts to a chain anchor, 30m/100'. Once the most popular route at the crag, this is still a very popular route. Climb straight up the slightly overhung wall passing just enough good holds to keep the pump at bay, and a small ledge to the top of the wall. ➤ Photo page 244.
FA: Louie Anderson, 1994.

K. Daily Java 12b★★★★
13 bolts to 2 open shuts, 30m/100'. A link-up. Start on *Daily Grind* and climb to its 9th bolt. After clipping this, climb up and left passing 2 independent bolts and some thin crimps. Connect with *Java* at its 11th bolt and finish on that route. If you're looking for a challenge, skip the left arete and ledge rests and enjoy the pump!
FA: Louie Anderson, 2001.

L. Daily Grind 12b★★★★
11 bolts to 2 open shuts, 30m/100'. The first completed route at the crag. This excellent route starts on the right arete of the face. A short ways up the arete climb left into a stemming corner and find rests where you can for the pumpy and powerful finish above.
FA: Louie Anderson, 1994.

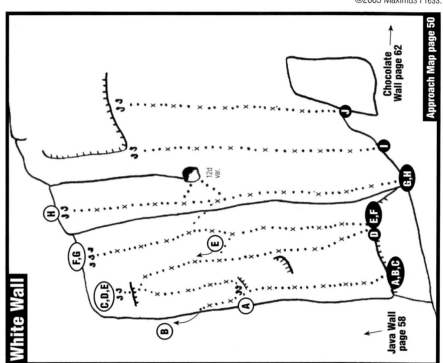

White Wall

Approach Map page 50

Chocolate Wall page 62

12d var.

Java Wall page 58

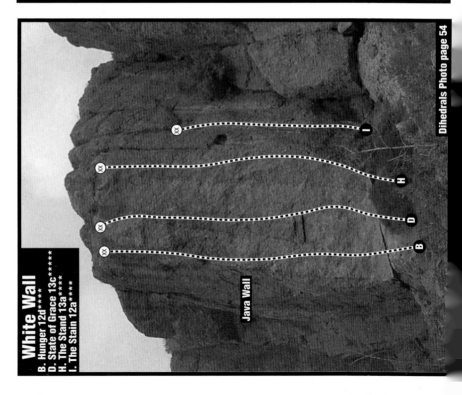

White Wall

B. Hunger 12d****
D. State of Grace 13c******
H. The Stand 13a****
I. The Stain 12a****

Dihedrals Photo page 54

Java Wall

Aron Couzens on **Booty** 12c****.

See Page 75

White Wall

Echo Cliffs Intro: Page 47. The best rock at the crag can be found on this wall, along with some of the best difficult routes in Southern California. All of the routes on the wall are long, steep and sustained. There is also a difficult open project waiting for anyone interested. These routes are only in the shade in the early morning and late afternoon.

A. Choptop 12c***
5 bolts to 2 open shuts. Scramble up onto the ledge and climb the left line of bolts to anchors mid-way up the wall.
FA: Louie Anderson, 1998.

B. The Hunger 12d****
10 bolts to 2 open shuts, 30m/100'. Climb *Choptop*, but instead of going to its anchors continue up the arete above, before finishing on its left face.
FA: Louie Anderson, 2002.

C. Legacy 14a? (open project)
9 bolts to shared 2 open shuts, 30m/100'. Climb *Choptop* and continue up the right line of bolts above, past a slopey hueco and thin crimps and pockets.
0B: Louie Anderson.

D. State of Grace 13c*****
8 bolts to shared 2 open shuts, 30m/100'. Amazing line up the center of the face. A true stamina route as most of the holds are larger than those usually found on a route of this rating. A little soft for the grade.
FA: Louie Anderson, 1998.

E. Expiration 13c****
9 bolts to shared 2 open shuts, 30m/100'. A link-up. Start on *Power of One* and after clipping its 5th bolt traverse left to finish on *State of Grace*.
FA: Louie Anderson, 1997.

F. The Power of One 13d*****
10 bolts to 3 open shuts, 30m/100'. One of the best routes in Southern California. Start off the ledge just to the right of *State of Grace* and climb past bouldery moves to the seam above and a committing deadpoint at the very end. ➤ Photo pages 42, 65.
FA: Louie Anderson, 1997.

G. One Night Stand 13b*****
10 bolts to 3 open shuts, 30m/100'. A link up. Start on *The Stand* and after clipping its 6th bolt climb left around the arete to finish on *The Power of One*. A fabulous route!
FA: Daniel Drazin, 2003.

H. The Stand 13a****
10 bolts to 2 open shuts, 30m/100'. Climbs up the right arete. Sequential moves lead to a tricky crux and easier climbing on the final headwall. For full credit (and the full rating) stay on the arete and away from the big hole off to the right.
➤ Front cover photo.
FA: Louie Anderson, 1998.

I. The Stain 12a****
7 bolts to 2 open shuts. Climbs the left of the two black streaks. Start up the steep and powerful bottom bulge to brilliant 5.11 climbing above. ➤ Photo page 68.
FA: Louie Anderson, 1996.

J. Double Standard 11b*
7 bolts to 2 open shuts. The right waterstreak unfortunately doesn't quite live up to its neighbor, however it does provide worthwhile climbing. Either stick clip the first bolt or stem up to clip it and then start from the ground. The back wall is off route.
FA: Louie Anderson, 1996.

Chocolate Wall

Echo Cliffs Intro: Page 47. Located to the right of the White Wall and just around the left arete of the Pink Wall, this wall offers fun climbing on a long, vertical face. These routes enjoy the morning shade.

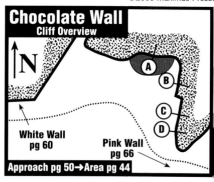

Chocolate Wall
Cliff Overview

White Wall
pg 60

Pink Wall
pg 66

Approach pg 50→Area pg 44

A. Calm 12a****

9 bolts to 2 open shuts. Starts on the slab left of the main Chocolate Wall and then climbs the amazing steep fin on a fine assortment of jugs with a single hard sequence. A wonderful route that is much steeper than it first appears.
➤ Photo this page.
FA: Doniel Drazin, 2000.

B. Bittersweet 10c***

4 bolts to 2 open shuts. Begins at the base of the slab and climbs over a small roof at the bottom and onto an intricate, technical and vertical face. Old School sport climbing.
FA: Louie Anderson, 2000.

C. Cookies and Cream 11b

8 bolts to shared open shuts. A contrived route that starts just left of *Death by Chocolate*. Clips the left line of bolts but ends up crowding and sharing the moves of that route.
FA: Jack Marshall, 1995.

D. Death by Chocolate 10d***

8 bolts to shared 2 open shuts. Turn the small roof just left of the right arete and climb the vertical face above. Once a very loose and scary route, its cleaned up a bunch in recent years due to continued traffic. Still a little "heady", but quite popular.
FA: Jack Marshall, 1995.

Jeff Truman on **Calm** 12a****. ©*Perri Nguyen Photo*

Doniel Drazin on **Here and Now** 12d***. ©*Perri Nguyen Photo.*

See Page 77

See Page 67

Will Chow on **Split Decision** 11d*****. ©*Perri Nguyen Photo*

See Page 61

Louie Anderson on **Power of One** 13d*****. ©*Perri Nguyen Photo.*

Pink Wall / Zombie Wall / Test Site

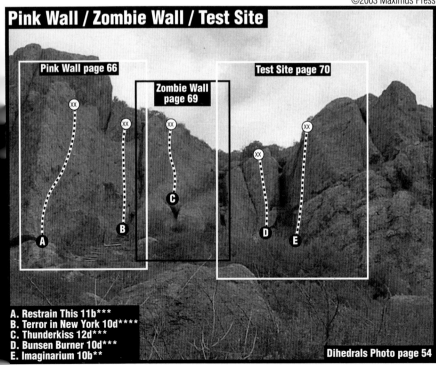

Pink Wall page 66

Test Site page 70

Zombie Wall page 69

A. Restrain This 11b***
B. Terror in New York 10d****
C. Thunderkiss 12d***
D. Bunsen Burner 10d***
E. Imaginarium 10b**

Dihedrals Photo page 54

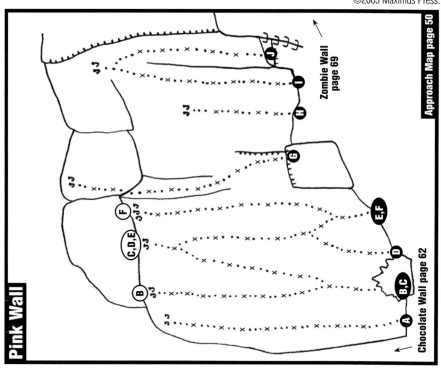

Pink Wall

Approach Map page 50

Zombie Wall page 69

Chocolate Wall page 62

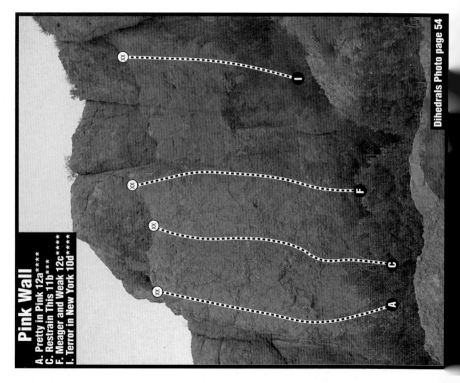

Pink Wall

A. Pretty in Pink 12a****
C. Restrain This 11b***
F. Meager and Weak 12c*****
I. Terror in New York 10d****

Dihedrals Photo page 54

Barry McWilliams on **Meager and Weak** 12c****.©*Perri Nguyen Photo.*

J. Sign of the Times 11b**

5 bolts to shared 2 open shuts. Begins off the ledge in the alcove above and to the right of *Terror in New York*. Climb the slightly overhung face to a high crux and an enjoyable slab finish.

FA: Louie Anderson, 2001.

Pink Wall

Echo Cliffs Intro: Page 47. This wall features a high concentration of routes on solid pink stone. Just about every route here is popular and is recommended. A great place to spend the second half of the day as the Pink Wall goes into the shade in the early afternoon.

A. Pretty in Pink 12a*****

8 bolts to 2 open shuts. Climbs the left arete to a heartbreaker crux move up high.

FA: Jack Marshall, 1995.

B. Split Decision 11d*****

10 bolts to 2 open shuts. Climbs relatively easy moves to the third bolt. From here climb up and left, encountering the crux almost right away. Continue past smallish holds and intriguing moves to the top of the wall. They don't get much better than this. ➤ Photo page 64.

FA: Jack Marshall, 1995.

C. Restrain This 11b***

8 bolts to shared 2 open shuts. Another very popular route. Begin as for *Split Decision*, but after clipping its 2nd bolt climb up and right through big holds and big moves to easier, lower angle moves and a pleasant stroll to the anchors.

FA: Jack Marshall, 1995.

D. Thinner 13a**

9 bolts to shared 2 open shuts. A short and powerful crux leads up and right to join *Pink Flamingo* at its 3rd bolt. Continue on that route to its anchors.

FA: Louie Anderson, 1998.

E. Pink Flamingo 12b***

8 bolts to shared 2 open shuts. Starts just to the right of the large bush and climbs up and right to the first bolt. After clipping this, set up as well as you can for a long span left and the beginning of the crux. A very pumpy route with no real stopper moves after the initial crux.

FA: Jack Marshall, 1995.

F. Meager and Weak 12c****

9 bolts to 3 open shuts. This fine route throws a little of everything at you along the way. Start as for *Pink Flamingo*, but after clipping its 1st bolt, climb slightly right and then straight up passing some big moves, some small pockets and some slopey holds. The block to the right is off route. ➤ Photo this page.

FA: Louie Anderson, 1996.

G. Cloud 9 10c*****

10 bolts to 2 open shuts, 30m/100'. This fine line sat unnoticed until 2001 when a new set of eyes looked at the cliff. Begin on top of the block at a small arete (or add an additional challenge by bouldering up the face of the block). Slowly trend up and left onto the left face of the dihedral and finally into very exposed stemming moves up high. An instant classic!

FA: Daniel Drazin, 2001.

H. Twist and Crawl 11a**

4 bolts to 2 open shuts. Climb over a powerful, but short bulge to the vertical face above.

FA: Louie Anderson, 1997.

I. Terror in New York 10d****

7 bolts to shared 2 open shuts. Enjoyable climbing between large holds. Climbs the tall face at the right end of the Pink Wall, passing a very cool sloping block down low.

FA: Louie Anderson, 2001.

Louie Anderson sticking the deadpoint on **Thunderkiss** 12d***. ©*Perri Nguyen Photo.*

Jeff Truman on **The Stain** 12a****. ©*Perri Nguyen Photo.*

See Page 61

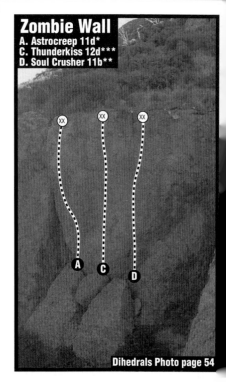

Zombie Wall
A. Astrocreep 11d*
C. Thunderkiss 12d***
D. Soul Crusher 11b**

Dihedrals Photo page 54

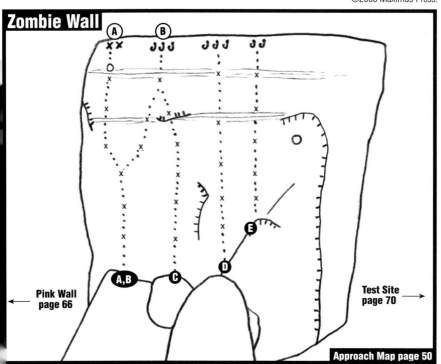

Zombie Wall

Pink Wall
page 66 ←

Test Site
page 70 →

Approach Map page 50

Zombie Wall

Echo Cliffs Intro: Page 47. The Zombie Wall was one of the first walls developed, but still hasn't seen much traffic. The routes here are steeper than they look, and should clean up nicely with some more traffic. The standout here is definitely *Thunderkiss*, which should be on your list if the grade is attainable. These routes are in the shade in the morning and late afternoon.

A. Astrocreep 11d*

bolts to a double biner anchor. This route starts at the far left end of the ledge. Climb straight up to a deep pocket and continue up the rounded buttress. After clipping the third bolt, go left through a dished section and climb the left headwall.
FA: Louie Anderson, 1995.

B. Psychoholic 12b**

bolts to shared triple shut anchor. Start as for *Astrocreep*, but after clipping the third bolt, climb up and right joining *Thunderkiss* at its last bolt.
FA: Louie Anderson, 1996.

C. Thunderkiss 12d***

6 bolts to shared triple shut anchor. The gem of the wall. An easy lower half leads to a mid height crux, followed by powerful pocket moves at the top. ➤ Photo facing page.
FA: Louie Anderson, 1995.

D. Soul Crusher 11b**

6 bolts to a triple shut anchor. This route leaves the ramp about five feet up and climbs a slightly overhung face at the bottom before turning technical and balancy above.
FA: Louie Anderson, 1995.

E. Knuckle Duster 11d*

5 bolts to a double shut anchor. Leave the ramp at its top and climb over a small bulge. Easier, but balancy climbing follows on the lower angled finish.
FA: Louie Anderson, 1995.

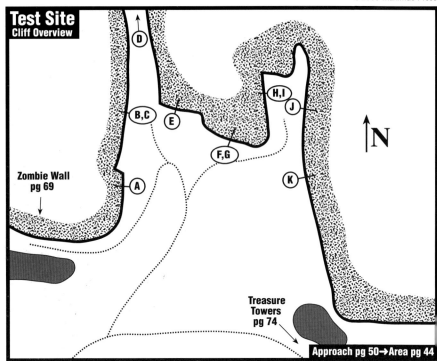

Test Site
Cliff Overview

D

H,I

J

B,C

E

F,G

Zombie Wall
pg 69

A

K

↑N

Treasure
Towers
pg 74

Approach pg 50→Area pg 44

Test Site

Echo Cliffs Intro: Page 47. The Test Site contains all of the routes found on the convoluted faces and corridors right of the Zombie Wall. Recently developed, this area offers one of the highest concentrations of moderate climbing at the crag. There is a lot of potential for new routes on the faces near *Imaginarium*. The Test Site enjoys mixed shade all day long.

A. Placebo 10a**
7 bolts to 2 open shuts. Follow the right facing flake. When it ends continue up the vertical face above.
FA: Doniel Drazin, 2003.

B. Catalyst 10b***
7 bolts to shared 2 open shuts. A link-up. Start on *Litmus Test*. After clipping the fourth bolt move up and left passing two independent bolts before joining *Placebo* at its last bolt.
FA: Doniel Drazin, 2003.

C. Litmus Test 10d****
6 bolts to 2 open shuts. This route begins eight feet right of *Placebo* and climbs diagonally up and right, following the line of *Simple Gully*. Unique moves.
➤ Photo facing page.
FA: Louie Anderson, 2001.

D. Simple Gully 5(x)
Free solo. This gully can be used to access the top of the cliff. Beware of the exposed stemming moves at the top; there have been several close calls here!

E. Test for Echo 11a*
4 bolts to 2 open shuts. Scramble up to the base and climb the low angle face just right of Simple Gully.
FA: Dean Goolsby, 1995.

F. Bunsen Burner 10d***
7 bolts to shared 2 open shuts. Climb up the bottom block (clipping one bolt) and continue climbing past its ledge. Follow the line of bolts up the center of the upper face.
FA: Doniel Drazin, 2001.

G. Buret Arete 11a**
7 bolts to shared 2 open shuts. Start as for *Bunsen Burner*, but after clipping its second bolt traverse right on the ledge and climb the steep arete before traversing bac to that route's anchors at the top.
FA: Doniel Drazin, 2001.

Craig Wilson on **Litmus Test** 10d****.

The next three routes are located in the hidden alcove up and right from *Bunsen Burner.*

H. Trial and Error 10b***

6 bolts to shared 2 open shuts. Climb up to a high first bolt. Turn the bulge and climb the slightly overhung face above on large edges.
FA: Louie Anderson, 2001.

I. Pop Quiz 10c**

6 bolts to shared 2 open shuts. Begin on *Trial and Error.* After clipping the first bolt of that route, climb up and right following the overhanging prow to its top. From here climb left to the last bolt of *Trial and Error,* finishing on that route.
FA: Louie Anderson, 2001.

J. Final Exam 11b**

5 bolts to 2 open shuts. Climb up the black face opposite *Trial and Error* passing several smooth cobbles at the top.
FA: Louie Anderson, 2002.

K. Imaginarium 10b**

6 bolts to 2 open shuts. Climb up the shallow dihedral before climbing up and right through a small bulge. Continue on the lower angled face above to the top of the wall.
FA: Louie Anderson, 2003.

See Page 77

Townsend Brown climbing the juggy roof of **Dogma** 11b***.

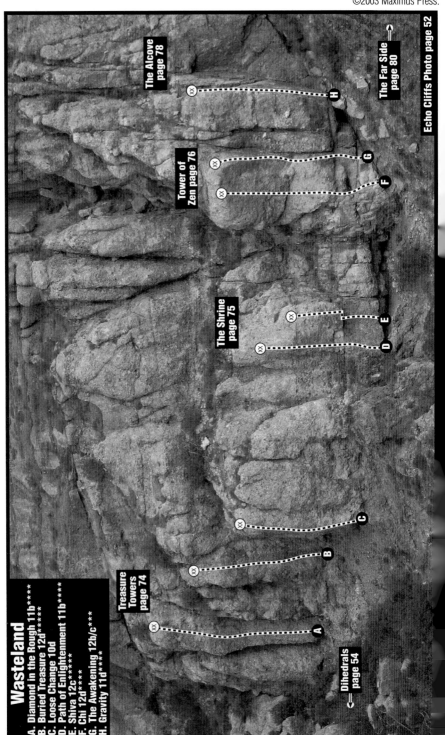

Wasteland

A. Diamond in the Rough 11b★★★★
B. Buried Treasure 12d★★★★★
C. Loose Change 10d
D. Path of Enlightenment 11b★★★★
E. Shiva 12c★★★★★
F. Chi 12d★★★★
G. The Awakening 12b/c★★★
H. Gravity 11d★★★★

The Alcove page 78

Tower of Zen page 76

The Shrine page 75

Treasure Towers page 74

Dihedrals page 54

The Far Side page 80

Echo Cliffs Photo page 52

Michel Leduff on **Windfall** 11a*****.

See Page 74

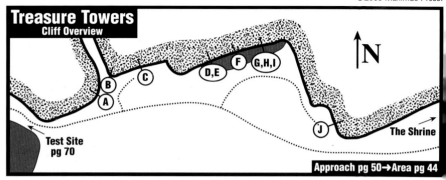

Treasure Towers
Cliff Overview

Test Site
pg 70

The Shrine

Approach pg 50→Area pg 44

Treasure Towers

Echo Cliffs Intro: Page 47. Originally dismissed as too chossy to bolt, these towers have yielded several fine routes. These have not come easily, however. All of the routes found here have seen multiple days of cleaning and are testaments to what a thorough cleaning can produce. Primarily stamina routes that are made up of sustained moves a few grades below the final rating in difficulty; they are wonderful training

routes for their grade. The Treasure Towers are in the shade in the morning and late afternoon.

A. The Pearl 11a**

7 bolts to 2 open shuts. Found on the left wall of the deep chimney, this route is much steeper than it looks. Climbs the vertical and slightly overhung face on a series of flat holds and cobbles to a steep finish.
FA: Louie Anderson, 2002.

B. Windfall 11a*****

8 bolts to 2 open shuts, 30m/100'. Climbs the right wall of the chimney up the steep, cobbled arete to a final bulge crux. ➤ Photo page 73.
FA: Louie Anderson, 2002.

C. Diamond in the Rough 11b****

11 bolts to 2 open shuts, 30m/100'. Start up the vertical water streak to a shallow, dished section at mid-route. From here, continue up and left onto the much steeper headwall. ➤ Photo page 28.
FA: Louie Anderson, 2002.

D. Scrapin' the Barrel 10c**

7 bolts to 2 shared open shuts, 30m/100'. Starts off the ledge 15 feet left of *Buried Treasure*. After clipping the second bolt, go up and left and climb the inside, right face of the water chute finishing on the vertical face to its right.
FA: Doniel Drazin, 2002.

E. Lucky Charms 12b***

8 bolts to shared 2 open shuts, 30m/100'. Begin as for *Scrapin' the Barrel*, but after clipping its second bolt continue up the overhung arete above before moving left at the end to finish at the anchors of that route. Very pumpy!
FA: Doniel Drazin, 2002.

F. Shakedown 14a? (project)

9 bolts to 2 open shuts, 30m/100'. Start just left of *Burie Treasure* and climb the lighter colored strip of rock. Very bouldery moves lead to a fun, steep finish.
OB: Doniel Drazin.

Treasure Towers

Wasteland Photo page 72

G. The Sting 13a/b★★★★

9 bolts to 2 open shuts, 30m/100'. A link up. Start on *Buried Treasure* and after clipping its 6th bolt, use sidepulls to climb left joining *Shakedown* at its 7th bolt.
FA: Doniel Drazin, 2003.

H. Buried Treasure 12d★★★★★

8 bolts to 2 open shuts, 30m/100'. Climb straight up the middle of the wall. The original route on the wall, this line showed what the tower had to offer. With no really hard single moves, and pretty good sized holds, this route is a true stamina challenge with an exciting finish.
FA: Louie Anderson, 1999.

I. Booty 12c★★★★

12 bolts to 2 open shuts, 30m/100'. Originally climbed as a much shorter, 5-bolt route in 1999, the first ascentionist returned and lengthened the route turning what was a good route into one of the best stamina routes at the crag. Start on *Buried Treasure* and at its second bolt, traverse right to the next line of bolts. Follow this to the top of the right pillar. For full credit, do not stem to the huge, right hand ramp at mid-height. Either skip the 2nd bolt or use a long draw to prevent rope drag. ➤ Photo page 61.
FA: Louie Anderson, 2002.

J. Loose Change 10d

8 bolts to 2 open shuts. Climbs the steep, cobbled face at the far right of the formation. Currently a test of the mind due to somewhat sketchy rock, however it will be great with some additional cleaning and traffic. Best described as a steeper version of the popular *Death by Chocolate*.
FA: Doniel Drazin, 2000.

The Shrine

Echo Cliffs Intro: Page 47. A beautiful pink face capped by roofs and bulges. These lines were always obvious, but for some reason did not get climbed until late in the development of the crag. They ended up being as good as they looked. The Shrine is in the shade in the early morning and in the afternoon.

K. Path of Enlightenment 1b★★★★

bolts to 2 open shuts. Begin climbing at the far left end of the ledge, near where the rock turns from pink to black. Climb up the corner system until it ends at a small bulge. After turning this follow the rounded arete above on fun holds.
FA: Doniel Drazin, 2003.

L. Buddha Belly 12b★★★★

bolts to 2 open shuts. Preclip the first bolt and then climb up the faint corner system to the left edge of the big roof. After clipping from the "belly" hold climb over the roof using a series of gastons and sidepulls to the cobbled face above. ➤ Photo this page.
FA: Louie Anderson, 2002.

The Shrine

Wasteland Photo page 72

M. Shiva 12c★★★★★

6 bolts to 2 open shuts. Preclip the first bolt and then climb straight up to the big roof. Climb the right edge of the roof and continue past large, flat holds above. Use a long draw on the roof bolt to prevent rope drag.
FA: Louie Anderson, 2002.

Steve Edwards on **Buddha Belly** 12b★★★★.

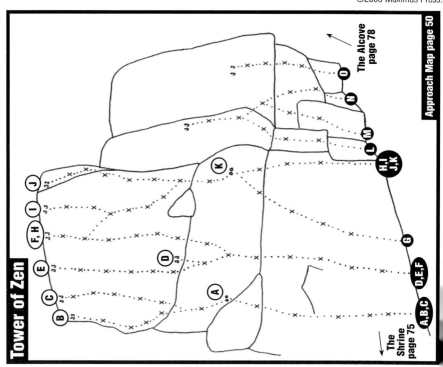

Tower of Zen

Approach Map page 50

The Alcove page 78

The Shrine page 75

Tower of Zen

C. Here and Now 12d***
F. Chi 12d****
J. The Awakening 12b/c***
M. Tantric Tango 11c**

Wasteland Photo page 72

Tower of Zen

Echo Cliffs Intro: Page 47. A dual purpose formation, the Tower of Zen offers both short, moderate routes at its base; and the option of continuing on these routes to link with more difficult climbing on the overhung headwall above. The longer route options are unfortunately lessened in quality one star by the presence of the mid-height slab and the no hands rest that it provides. These routes are in the shade in the morning and late afternoon.

A. Daily Practice 11a**

5 bolts to a double carabiner anchor on a ledge. Climb the slightly overhung stemming scoop and then through the ledged face above.

FA: Doniel Drazin, 2002.

B. 4 Moves to Happiness 12a**

11 bolts to 2 open shuts, 30m/100'. Climb *Daily Practice* and continue past its anchors until you can climb over the short bulge above. From here climb the left bolt line up a very steep (and unfortunately short) bulge above. The moves on the bulge make it all worthwhile.

➤ Photo page 63.

FA: Doniel Drazin, 2002.

C. Here and Now 12d***

12 bolts to 2 open shuts, 30m/100'. Climb *Daily Practice* and continue past its anchors until you can climb over the short bulge above. From here climb the right bolt line passing two large cobbles and a devious crux sequence. A very pumpy route that demands attention right to the end.

FA: Doniel Drazin, 2002.

D. Simplicity 10c**

7 bolts to 2 open shuts. Follow a series of corners to the short pocketed bulge above. After turning this continue up the slab above following the left bolt line to the anchors. Long draws on bolts #4 and #7 will help prevent rope drag.

FA: Doniel Drazin, 2002.

E. Spontaneous Wisdom 12b****

12 bolts to 2 open shuts, 30m/100'. Climb *Simplicity* and after clipping its last bolt continue climbing up and left onto the steep headwall face above. A fun dyno hits you right near the end.

FA: Louie Anderson, 2002.

F. Chi 12d****

13 bolts to 2 open shuts, 30m/100'. Climb *Simplicity*, after clipping its 6th bolt climb up and right clipping one more bolt before charging up the headwall, passing just enough large holds to keep the pump at bay before encountering the crux.

FA: Doniel Drazin, 2002.

G. Project ?

4 bolts to a double carabiner anchor.

EB: Doniel Drazin.

H. Mantra 12d***

12 bolts to 2 open shuts, 30m/100'. A link up. Climb *Meditation Station* to its 10th bolt and then traverse the rail left to join *Chi* at its 12th bolt. Finish on this route.

FA: Doniel Drazin, 2002.

I. Meditation Station 12c***

12 bolts to 2 open shuts, 30m/100'. Climb *Comfort Zone* and when you reach its anchors continue up the slab above. At the top of the slab climb left following a ramp onto the steep headwall. A big toss in the middle of the headwall provides the excitement on this popular route. Big moves between big holds.

FA: Doniel Drazin, 2002.

J. The Awakening 12b/c***

11 bolts to 2 open shuts, 30m/100'. Climb *Comfort Zone*, when you reach its anchors continue up the slab above. At the top of

the slab climb the right line of bolts up the overhanging arete and move right to finish on the vertical face above.

FA: Louie Anderson, 2001.

K. Comfort Zone 11c***

3 bolts to a double carabiner anchor. Start off the trail and climb up to an obvious pocket in the middle of the blank face. After a deadpoint crux climb up and left over the bulge to the anchors. Could be more difficult if under 5' 10".

FA: Louie Anderson, 2001.

L. Karma Cowboy 12d***

5 bolts to shared 2 open shuts. Start with both hands on the flat shelf and climb over a small roof and then up the vertical face to the pocketed roof above. A hard toss to the jug at the lip leads to the headwall.

FA: Louie Anderson, 2002.

M. Tantric Tango 11c**

5 bolts to shared 2 open shuts. Preclip the first bolt and then climb up the flake in the corner to large pockets below a bulge. Throw to the jug over the bulge and continue stemming up the corner above.

FA: Louie Anderson, 2002.

N. Dogma 11b***

5 bolts to shared 2 open shuts. Start matched on the sloping edge and throw to the horizontal rail under the roof. After clipping the first bolt climb through the roof on deep pockets before traversing left and finishing in the stemming corner of *Tantric Tango*. ➤ Photo page 71.

FA: Louie Anderson, 2002.

O. Dean's Route 12b*

4 bolts out steep cave to 2 open shuts. Start by clipping the first bolt and stepping off the large boulder above the cave. Climb over the short bulge using deep pockets and continue up the headwall passing hidden jugs. A direct start in the cave below is possible at a harder grade.

FA: Dean Goolsby, 1998.

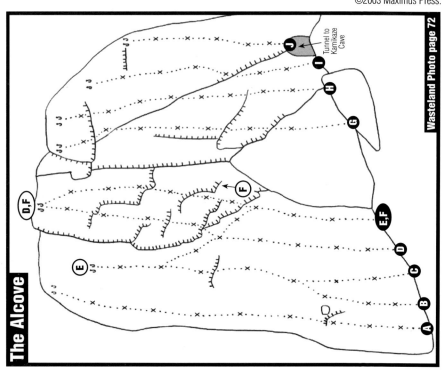

The Alcove

Wasteland Photo page 72

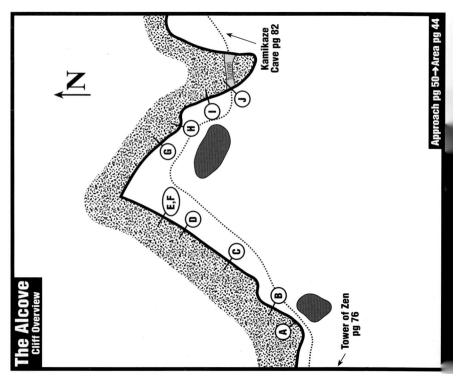

The Alcove
Cliff Overview

Approach pg 50→Area pg 44

Kamikaze Cave pg 82

Tower of Zen pg 76

The Alcove

Echo Cliffs Intro: Page 47. Located uphill and around the corner from the Tower of Zen, The Alcove offers slightly overhung routes that tend to have somewhat smaller holds than others of their grade at Echo. The Alcove is also home to the one and only crack line at the Crag, *The Guillotine*. The Alcove routes are in the shade in the afternoon, and the routes on the right wall are also in the shade in the morning.

Many link-ups are possible combining routes A, B and C. All are enjoyable and roughly the same grade.

A. Gravity 11d★★★★
9 bolts to 2 open shuts, 30m/100'. Start off the flat boulder with both hands matched on a flake. A big move up and left starts the fun. Climb through some bulges and then up the arete using a variety of moves. ➤ Photo page 46.
FA: Louie Anderson, 2002.

B. Whippersnapper 12a★★★
8 bolts to shared 2 open shuts. The direct start to *Geezer*. Begin just to the right of *Gravity*, stepping off the reinforced section of the trail. A steep start past large holds leads to a short traverse right to join Geezer at its 3rd bolt.
FA: Louie Anderson, 2002.

C. Geezer 12a★★★
7 bolts to shared 2 open shuts. Climb edges and crimps up the center of the face diagonalling up and left towards a hueco below a bulge. After the bulge the difficulty of the climbing eases.
FA: Louie Anderson, 1997.

D. Pride 13a★★★★
9 bolts to shared 2 open shuts. The crimp route at Echo. Climb straight up, on thin edges and crimps to a rest at the flake. Cross over the flake and continue on small holds to the top of the wall.
FA: Louie Anderson, 1997.

E. The Guillotine 10b★★
8 bolts to shared 2 open shuts. Starts up the corner, clipping the bolts on the left wall. Once you reach the flake follow it up and left to *Geezer's* anchors.
FA: Louie Anderson, 1997.

F. Carnivore 12b★★★
9 bolts to shared 2 open shuts. Begin as for *The Guillotine*, but once the flake is reached cross over it and continue up the steep black water streak. ➤ Photo this page.
FA: Louie Anderson, 1997.

G. El Niño 11c★★★
7 bolts to 2 open shuts. Easy entry moves lead to a steeper headwall. Climb up this wall using sidepulls and flat edges to meet a diagonal crack at mid-route. Follow this to and then climb over the small roof at the top of the wall. A popular route.
FA: Louie Anderson, 1997.

H. Project ?
8 bolts to 2 open shuts. Step over onto the slab left of *The Right Stuff* and climb up the line of bolts above.
EB: Dean Goolsby.

I. The Right Stuff 12d★★
6 bolts to 2 open shuts. Start just left of the tunnel and climb up and left under a bulge. Climb over the bulge using incut holds and continue past many small holds and a mono on the vertical wall above.
FA: Louie Anderson, 1997.

J. Spam 12b
5 bolts to 2 open shuts. Climb directly above the tunnel. Pull onto the face using large pockets. Continue up the vertical face and finish on the right arete.
FA: Louie Anderson, 1997.

Diana Jew on **Carnivore** 12b★★★.

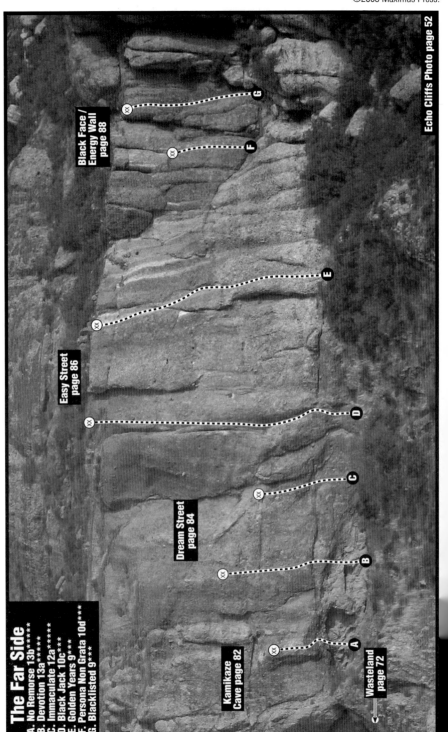

Echo Cliffs Photo page 52

Black Face / Energy Wall page 88

Easy Street page 86

Dream Street page 84

Kamikaze Cave page 82

Wasteland page 72

The Far Side
A. No Remorse 13b*****
B. Devotion 13a*****
C. Immaculate 12a******
D. Black Jack 10c***
E. Golden Years 9***
F. Persona Non Grata 10d***
G. Blacklisted 9***

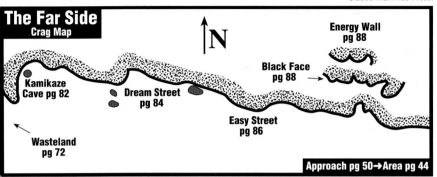

The Far Side
Crag Map

N

Energy Wall
pg 88

Black Face
pg 88 →

Kamikaze
Cave pg 82

Dream Street
pg 84

Easy Street
pg 86

Wasteland
pg 72

Approach pg 50→Area pg 44

Angelo Ghiglieri on **Hijacked** 12b****. ©Ryan Wedemeyer Photo.

See Page 83

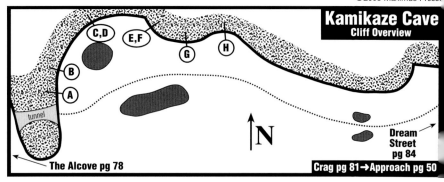

Kamikaze Cave

Echo Cliffs Intro: Page 47. The Kamikaze cave offers the steepest rock found at the crag, as well as some of the more popular routes. The steep jugs found on some of the routes here allow for quick redpoints by the strong. The cave offers mixed shade in the morning and complete shade in the afternoon.

Doniel Drazin on **No Remorse** 13b*****. *Chris Brewer Photo*

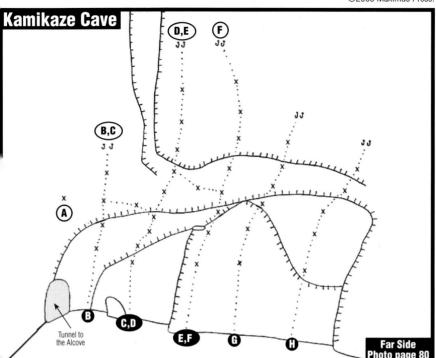

Kamikaze Cave

Tunnel to
the Alcove

**Far Side
Photo page 80**

Kamikaze Cave

A. Open Project ??
The lonely bolt up over the roof.

B. The Gimp 13a**
bolts to 2 open shuts. Climb past rounded jugs to a sequential roof, and finally through a powerful headwall section. There is an optional sit start if you want to up the ante.
FA: Louie Anderson, 1995.

C. Ruckus 13c***
bolts to 2 open shuts. A link-up. Climb the first 4 bolts of Kamikaze and then cut left across the lip of the roof, passing 1 independent bolt to join The Gimp at its 3rd bolt.
FA: Louie Anderson, 1996.

D. Kamikaze 14a/b****
bolts to 2 open shuts. Ultra steep pocket climbing leads to a strenuous undercling sequence just before the lip. Then a devious boulder problem guards passage to the headwall above. Currently the hardest route in the Santa Monicas.
FA: Louie Anderson, 1996.

E. Zero ?? (project)
9 bolts to 2 open shuts. Starts on No Remorse and climbs that route to its 4th bolt. After clipping this, climb left passing one independent bolt to join Kamikaze at its 6th bolt. Finish on that route.
OB: Louie Anderson.

F. No Remorse 13b*****
8 bolts to 2 open shuts. Archetypical cave route. Start up the slightly overhung base pedestal and then climb up through the roof using underclings, toe cams, heel and toe hooks, kneebars and whatever else works. Once you reach the lip, catch a quick shake and continue up the headwall passing a final challenge to the anchors. One of the best at the crag! ➤ Photo page 53, facing page.
FA: Louie Anderson, 1999.

G. Crash and Burn 12d*****
6 bolts to 2 open shuts. Steep jugs—what more could you ask for? Maybe a "how bad do you want it?" move at the end? Extremely popular. ➤ Photo page 230.
FA: Louie Anderson, 1998.

H. Hijacked 12b****
5 bolts to 2 open shuts. Climbs through a scooped entry section and then up and right; diagonally, through the big roof via positive pockets and huecos. Very popular.
➤ Photo pages 11, 81.
FA: Louie Anderson, 2000.

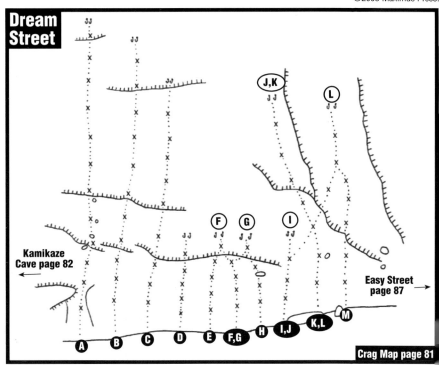

Dream Street

Kamikaze Cave page 82 ←

Easy Street page 87 →

Crag Map page 81

Dream Street

Echo Cliffs Intro: Page 47. Home to some of the hardest routes at the crag, Dream Street still has limited potential for further development, and has an open project that should check in somewhere in the middle of the 5.14 grade. It's all yours if you're interested. Other than the first routes listed, these routes are short by Echo standards and are very powerful. The Dream Street routes are in the shade in the early morning and from mid afternoon on.

A. Devotion 13a*****

12 bolts to 2 open shuts, 30m/100'. Often compared to *Joe Six Pack* in the Virgin River Gorge, this awesome line climbs through two steep bulges, using brilliant sequences, before encountering the vertical and pumpy headwall. At the top of this headwall you can thankfully catch a good rest before dealing with the final bulge.
FA: Doniel Drazin, 2001.

B. Apathy 12d****

11 bolts to 2 open shuts, 30m/100'. Amazingly good climbing on the lower half of this route unfortunately leads to easier climbing on the headwall. Still a great and very popular route. A pretty quick send if you can do the lower crux. ➤ Photo facing page.
FA: Louie Anderson, 2000.

C. The One and Only ?? (project)

9 bolts to 2 open shuts, 30m/100'. Climb the smooth gre face 6 feet right of *Apathy*, with a pocket crux low and a thin crimp crux on the upper headwall.
OB: Louie Anderson.

D. The Almighty 14? (open project)

5 bolts to 2 open shuts. Blocky holds lead to widely spaced pockets.
EB: Louie Anderson.

E. Prodigy 13d/14a***

5 bolts to 2 open shuts. After the highly featured start, climb past a series of powerful and shouldery sidepulls and gastons.
FA: Louie Anderson, 1996.

F. Axis of Evil 13b/c***

5 bolts to shared 2 open shuts. This route starts at a head high oval hueco. Powerful pocket moves lead up the steep face. After clipping the 4th bolt climb left to clip the last bolt of *Prodigy* and finish on that route.
FA: Mike Nash, 2003. OB: Louie Anderson.

G. The Brute 13a**

4 bolts to 2 open shuts. A link-up. An alternate finish to *Axis of Evil*. After clipping the 4th bolt of that route climb up and right to finish on the final bulge of *Brutal Bypass*.
FA: Louie Anderson, 1997.

H. Brutal Bypass 12d**

4 bolts to 2 open shuts. Climbs thin pockets, followed by a toss to the big shelf. From here climb up and left over the bulge.
FA: Louie Anderson, 1998.

I. Super Tick 12b*

3 bolts to 2 open shuts. A short and bouldery route that climbs to and past a baseball sized slopey pocket.
FA: Louie Anderson, 1996.

J. Super Mac 12b***

8 bolts to 2 open shuts. A link-up. Start on *Super Tick* and climb to its 3rd bolt before heading right to finish up *Immaculate*. Either use a long sling on the 3rd bolt of *Super Tick* or unclip it after clipping the next bolt.
FA: Doniel Drazin, 1999.

K. Immaculate 12a*****

7 bolts to 2 open shuts. Everything the name implies. Climbs the beautiful, smooth face up to and over a small bulge. Finishes up the water polished, black headwall.
FA: Louie Anderson, 1998.

L. Immaculate Annihilation 12a****

6 bolts to 2 open shuts. A link-up. Climb *Immaculate* to its 3rd bolt before heading right passing 1 independent bolt to join *Annihilator* at its 6th bolt.
FA: Louie Anderson, 1998.

M. Annihilator 11d****

7 bolts to 2 open shuts. After some fun moves on the golden face, climb up a flake and over some small roofs to finish on the pumpy headwall.
FA: Louie Anderson, 1998.

Michel Leduff approaching the next bulge on **Apathy** 12d****.

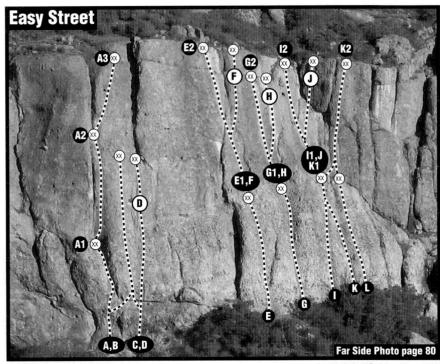

Easy Street

Far Side Photo page 80

Kayla Anderson on the 1st pitch of **Golden Years** 6★★

Easy Street

Echo Cliffs Intro: Page 47. The home of long moderates. There is still considerable potential here for more routes. All of the remaining lines promise to be just as good as those already completed and of similar grades. These routes are in the shade in the early morning and from mid afternoon on. With a shady base and multi-pitch climbing, *Easy Street* offers one of the finest collections of moderate sport climbs in Southern California.

A. Blackjack 10c★★★

The first multi-pitch route at the crag.
Pitch 1: 10b★★★. 7 bolts to 2 open shuts (or continue to 2 ring anchors on the ledge above if you plan on climbing the upper pitches). Climb the slightly overhung face using large holds to reach the water chute above. A very popular warm-up route.
Pitch 2: 10c★★★★. 7 bolts to 2 ring anchors. An amazing pitch that follows granite-like crimps and edges up the vertical headwall.
Pitch 3: 8. 7 bolts to 2 ring anchors on the summit. Climbs the slab up to and over a small overlap. Really only worthwhile to access the top or to say you've done the whole route.
FA: Louie Anderson, Doniel Drazin, 2000.

B. Blackout 10c★★★★

14 bolts to 2 open shuts, 30m/100'. A link-up. Begin as for *Blackjack*, but after clipping its 3rd bolt hand traverse right on the large flake and clip an independent bolt (once this is clipped, you may want to unclip the previous bolt to reduce rope drag). Continue right to join *Dugout* at its 3rd bolt. A slightly more difficult start than the regular route.
FA: Doniel Drazin, 2001.

C. Dugout 10c★★★★

12 bolts to 2 open shuts, 30m/100'. Begin as for *Casey at the Bat*, but after clipping its 1st bolt climb left and follow the line of bolts over small bulges, up an amazing buttress filled with edges of all sizes.
FA: Doniel Drazin, 2001.

D. Casey at the Bat 10b★★★★★

11 bolts to 2 open shuts, 30m/100'. Starts 10 feet to the right of *Blackjack* at the foot of a small hill. Climb the short face up to a small roof. After turning this roof continue up easier and very enjoyable moves to an anchor high on the wall. One of the best 5.10's at the crag and a very popular route.
FA: Doniel Drazin, 2000.

E. Golden Years 9★★★

Pitch 1: 6★★. 6 bolts to 2 ring anchors on the ledge above. Climb the water chute. ➤ Photo facing page.
Pitch 2: 9★★★. 9 bolts to 2 open shuts, 30m/100'. Climb over the small bulge and follow the gold water streak as it wanders up the slab and left over a seam onto steeper terrain.
FA: Louie Anderson, 2001.

F. Dirty Deeds 8★★★★

9 bolts to 2 open shuts, 30m/100'. Begin as for *Golden Years'* second pitch, but after clipping its 3rd bolt climb up and right onto the steeper buttress.
FA: Louie Anderson, 2001.

G. The Serpent 10a★★★★

Pitch 1: 6★★. 8 bolts to a double ring anchor on the ledge. Climb up the next water chute to the right of *Golden Years*.
Pitch 2: 10a★★★★. 8 bolts to 2 open shuts. Pull over the steep bulge and continue on the face above, following the left water streak on amazing rock.
FA: Loie Anderson, 2003.

H. Watermark 9★★★

8 bolts to 2 open shuts. Begin as for *The Serpent's* second pitch, but after clipping its 3rd bolt traverse up and right and follow the right water streak.
FA: Louie Anderson, 2003.

I. Righteous Babe 8★★★

Pitch 1: 7★★★. 8 bolts to a double biner anchor on the ledge. This route climbs the obvious wide, black water streak to the right of *The Serpent*.
Pitch 2: 8★★★. 8 bolts to 2 open shuts. Pull onto the slab above the anchors and climb it up to the final headwall.
FA: Traci Marx, Doniel Drazin, 2003.

J. Hippie Chick 10c★★

9 bolts to 2 open shuts. Begin as for *Righteous Babe's* second pitch, but after clipping its 4th bolt climb up and right finishing up the steep face.
FA: Doniel Drazin, Louie Anderson, 2003.

K. Head Wound 9★★★★

Pitch 1: 7★★. 9 bolts to a double biner anchor. This route follows the water groove just right of *Righteous Babe*, sharing that route's last bolt.
Pitch 2: 9★★★★. 9 bolts to 2 open shuts. Starts by heading up and right, then climbs the orange face filled with square cut edges; getting steeper and harder as you get higher. An incredible pitch on great rock!
FA: Doniel Drazin, 2003.

L. Rockhopper 7★

9 bolts to a double biner anchor. Start 15 feet right of *Head Wound* and climb up the pocketed face. Can also be used to approach *Head Wound's* 2nd pitch.
FA: Louie Anderson, 2003.

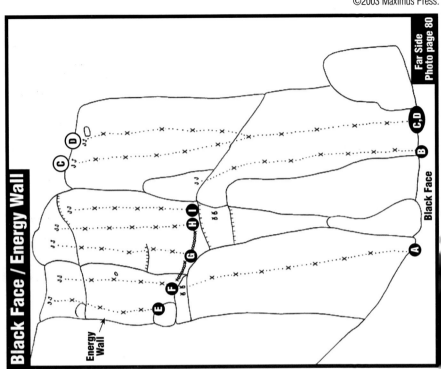

Black Face / Energy Wall

Far Side
Photo page 80

Black Face

Energy
Wall

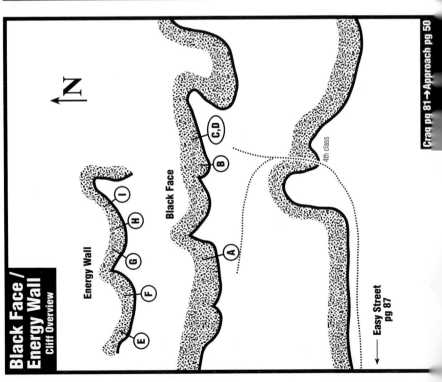

**Black Face /
Energy Wall**
Cliff Overview

N

Energy Wall

Black Face

Easy Street
pg 87

4th class

Crag pg 81 →Approach pg 50

Rachel Coleman on **Blacklisted** 9***.

H. Whoop Ass 11c***

5 bolts to 2 open shuts. If you like thin crimps, this is your route. Climbs past crimpy moves on a beautifully polished, orange face.

FA: Louie Anderson, 2001.

I. Red Bull 10d**

4 bolts to 2 open shuts. Looks harder than it really is. Climb up the far right side of the face passing a large sloper to incut edges and the end of the route.

FA: Louie Anderson, 2001.

Black Face

Echo Cliffs Intro: Page 47. The Black Face marks the farthest right boundary of the current route development, however there is still potential for routes farther down the cliffline. This face offers some wonderful moderate routes on polished black rock. The Black Face terrace is approached via an easy 4th class scramble for 35 feet from the main base trail. The routes on this wall are in the shade in the early morning and from mid afternoon on.

A. Persona Non Grata 10d***

7 bolts to 2 ring anchors on the ledge above. After a powerful initial sequence, enjoy vertical moves on fun holds to the top of the wall. This is the popular approach to the Energy Wall routes above.

FA: Louie Anderson, 2001.

B. Black Crack 8**

7 bolts to 2 open shuts. Climb up the obvious crack until it is possible to step right onto the face. From here continue up easier terrain using large flat holds. Can be used to access the Energy Wall routes above.

FA: Louie Anderson, 2000.

C. Blacklisted 9***

10 bolts to 2 open shuts, 30m/100'. Start just a few feet to the right of *Black Crack* and after the steep start, enjoy the less than vertical middle section before dealing with the final headwall. ➤ Photo this page.

FA: Louie Anderson, 2000.

D. Blackballed 10b***

10 bolts to 2 open shuts, 30m/100'. Begin as for *Blacklisted*, but after clipping its 5th bolt, climb up and right to a harder headwall finish and separate anchors.

FA: Daniel Drazin, 2000.

Energy Wall

Located on the ledge system above the Black Face routes, the Energy Wall offers short, powerful routes on some very high quality rock. It can be approached by climbing either *Persona Non Grata* or *Black Crack*. These routes are also in the shade in the early morning and from mid afternoon on.

E. Ginseng Giant 11b**

4 bolts to 2 open shuts. Start off a small ramp at the far left of the wall. Climb past cool pocket-like features on some of the best rock at the crag to a mid height crux. Finishes on easier terrain.

FA: Louie Anderson, 2001.

F. Energy 12a***

4 bolts to 2 open shuts. Climb up large holds to the first bolt and get ready for the crux. A short, powerful route on perfect rock! Best to belay from a hanging stance set up off one of the chains.

FA: Louie Anderson, 2001.

G. Jolt 12a***

5 bolts to 2 open shuts. Starts at the left side of the right-hand face and climbs slightly overhung rock, past some powerful moves. Continue past a final bolt on the headwall above to the anchors.

FA: Louie Anderson, 2001.

©2003 Maximus Press.

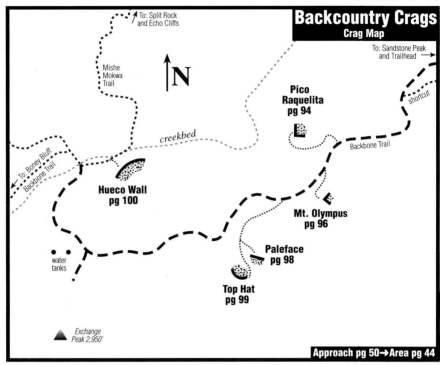

Approach pg 50→Area pg 44

Backcountry Crags

The individual crags found in this area are among the newest developments found in the guide. Most were established in 2001 and 2002 and represent some of the first forays into the vast potential found in this section of the Santa Monicas. This basin is filled with cliffs of varying sizes, including formations up to 200 feet in height. While there are rumors of other routes in the area, currently no information is available.

Backcountry Crags Details

Elevation: 2,700 ft.
Exposure: Varied, sun and shade.
Sport Climbs: 41 routes, 5.7 to 12d.
Drive From Hwy 101: 20 minutes.
Drive From Hwy 1: 15 minutes
Approach: 35 to 70 minute hike.

The Approach: Map page 50. *Ventura Freeway (101):* Exit the freeway at the Westlake Blvd. (23 South) exit and head south (towards the ocean). You will pass through a couple of traffic signals before coming to a stop sign at Potrero Rd. (mile 1.6 from the 101). Continue through this stop sign, passing a large rock formation on your right until you reach another stop sign at Carlisle Canyon Rd. (mile 2.7). Drive straight through this intersection and follow the road as it winds up through the hills. At mile 4.7 you will merge with Mulholland Dr., which comes in from your left. Continue on through this intersection until you reach a stop sign (at mile 6.4), with Mulholland Dr. continuing on your right. Turn here and then turn right again onto Little Sycamore

Canyon Rd. (mile 6.7). This road will wind through the hills, changing name to Yerba Buena Rd. and passing a small development of homes at a sharp left turn in the road (mile 8.5) and the Mishe Mokwa trailhead (mile 10.3) until you reach the trailhead at mile 10.9. A short uphill dirt drive will lead to the upper parking area.

Pacific Coast Highway (1): From Pacific Coast Hwy., head inland on Yerba Buena Rd. (located adjacent to Neptune's Net restaurant). Head up into the hills, passing a junction with Cortharin Rd. after 2.9 miles. At 3.8 miles you will pass the Circle X Ranger Station on your right and at 4.8 miles you will see the short uphill dirt drive leading up to the upper parking area and the trailhead. The trail starts directly from the north end of the parking area.

Decker Road (23): You can also leave Pacific Coast Hwy. (1) and head inland on Decker Road (23 North). Follow this road for 4.8 miles until you reach a stop sign at Mulholland Dr., which comes in from your left. Turn left here and continue to a right turn onto Little Sycamore Canyon Rd. (mile 5.1 from Pacific Coast Hwy.). This road will wind through the hills, changing name to Yerba Buena Rd. and passing a small development of homes at a sharp left turn in the road (mile 6.9) and the Mishe Mokwa trailhead (mile 8.7) until you reach the trailhead at mile 9.3. A short uphill dirt drive will lead to the upper parking area. The trail starts directly from the north end of the parking area.

From the Trailhead: Follow the steep fire road that leaves from the north end of the parking area. At approximately 0.3 miles you will reach a junction with the Mishe Mokwa connector trail on your right. Continue on the main fire road to Sandstone Peak. From here either continue on the fire road down to your right (if riding bikes) or head down a shortcut footpath straight ahead from the uphill approach fire road. This footpath will join up with the main fire road after a few minutes, but will save at least five minutes of hiking time. Shortly after rejoining the fire road you will encounter a sharp left hand turn in the road leading to a steep descent section, where the road is covered with chain-link fencing for improved traction. From here refer to the following instructions for the individual cliffs.

Pico Raquelita: The approach trail to the crag leaves the fire road just before going down this steep section of road. Continue straight ahead from the fire road (instead of turning left and heading down the road) and follow a footpath as it heads left downhill and then back to the right. Within minutes you should reach a broad apron of rock. Continue across this rock, traversing around the left side of the formation. After a few minutes this apron will end and you will be faced with another rock formation with its steep side facing you. Hike downhill to the left (around a big bush) and continue traversing the hill and crossing some small slabby sections of rock until you reach an obvious blocky formation. Approximately 40-60 minutes hiking time.

Mount Olympus: After crossing the chain-link section of road, an obvious cobbled tower will be seen on your left and slightly downhill from the fire road. This is Mount Olympus. A footpath leaves the fire road and leads to the tower. Approximately 35-55 minutes hiking time.

Paleface and Top Hat: After crossing the chain-link section of road, you will pass an obvious cobbled tower on your left (Mount Olympus). A few minutes after passing the tower you will come to a wide saddle, offering views of the valley below and the Pacific Ocean beyond. A large wall is facing directly back at you). This is the Paleface wall and the smaller formations on the summit above are the Top Hat. A footpath leaves the saddle on the right and leads to the formations. To approach Paleface from this footpath, head down a rocky slab to it's base. Approximately 45-65 minutes hiking time.

Hueco Wall: After crossing the chain-link section of road, you will pass an obvious cobbled tower on your left (Mount Olympus). Continue on the fire road, passing several more formations until you reach a junction with another fire road (heading uphill on your left). You will see a pair of water tanks on the hillside up and left. Follow the right hand road (leading downhill) until it flattens out and you reach another junction with a trail on your left. Continue straight ahead until you reach an obvious dry creekbed. Follow this creekbed to the right, passing under an old water pipe, until just before you reach two large boulders on your right. Just before the first boulder a faint trail leaves the creekbed on your right. As you near the crag, the trail become more obvious and the bushes denser. Approximately 50-70 minutes hiking time.

See Page 107 Louie Anderson on the steep prow of **Lithium** 13c*** at Boney Bluff. ©*Perri Nguyen Photo.*

Pico Raquelita
A. 101 10a**
B. Up Chuck 12a**
C. Humdinger 11c***
D. Zinger 12d***
E. Splitter 10c***
F. Whizbang 12b***
G. Short and Spicy 11d***
H. Hinge 11a*

approach

Crag Map page 90

Pico Raquelita

Backcountry Crags Intro: Page 90. A
short little wall that allows for fun
climbing and the only clean crack route
found so far in this area of the Santa
Monicas. The climbs are short, but are
generally very sustained for their grade.
All routes are in the shade in the
morning and are described right to left
as they are approached.

There is potential for a good
bouldering circuit on the boulders below
the main crag. The rock is very solid and
would require only minimal cleaning to
establish several problems on their
steep faces and ultra steep caves.

The first three routes listed are
found on the face right of the prominent
arete.

A. 101 10a**
3 bolts to a double ring anchor. A fun warm-up route that
follows the shallow corner at the right side of the face.
FA: Jong Long, Joe Kristy, Kelly Corcorran, 2002.

B. Up Chuck 12a**
3 bolts to a double ring and biner anchor. This route
begins just left of *101* and climbs up and left following a
series of pockets to a high crux.
FA: John Long, Joe Kristy, Kelly Corcorran, 2002.

C. Humdinger 11c***
3 bolts to a double ring anchor just over the lip. An
interesting route that starts at the base of the arete and
climbs its left side before moving onto the overhanging
right face. This route consists of long moves between
positive holds. ➤ Photo facing page.
FA: Louie Anderson, 2002. FTR: John Long.

The remaining routes are found on the
left side of the prominent arete and
climb stone that is among the best four
in the Santa Monicas; comparing to tha
found on the White Wall of Echo Cliffs
and at The Lookout.

D. Zinger 12d***
3 bolts to 2 open shuts. Start as for *Humdinger*, but aft
clipping its first bolt continue up the steep left side of t
arete passing several thin crimps at the end.
FA: Louie Anderson, 2002.

E. Splitter 10c***

ear to 4", a 2 bolt anchor lies on the slab above, just
elow the summit boulder. Climbs the ultra-clean and
nooth crack up the overhanging wall on locker jams and
ebacks.
A: Bill Leventhal, 2002. FTR: John Long.

F. Whizbang 12b***

bolts to 2 shared open shuts. Begin climbing at a
aseball sized pocket and follow a series of edges and
depulls up and left.
: Louie Anderson, 2002.

G. Short and Spicy (S&S) 11d***

3 bolts to 2 shared open shuts. Start climbing at the left
arete and climb up and right to finish in the shallow
dihedral above.
FA: Louie Anderson, 2002.

H. Hinge 11a*

3 bolts to a double chain anchor on the ledge above.
Climbs the left side of the far left arete. A strenuous,
overhanging "hinge" job.
FA: Louie Anderson, 2002. FTR: John Long.

Matt Callender on **Humdinger** 11c***. *Mark Donovan Photo.*

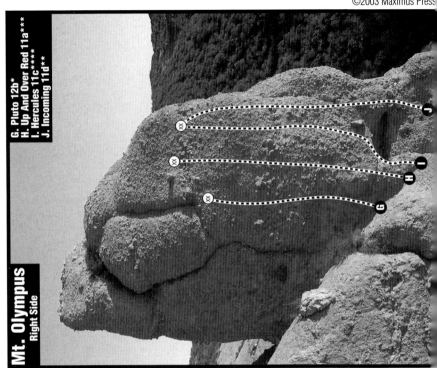

Mt. Olympus
Right Side

G. Pluto 12b*
H. Up And Over Red 11a***
I. Hercules 11c****
J. Incoming 11d**

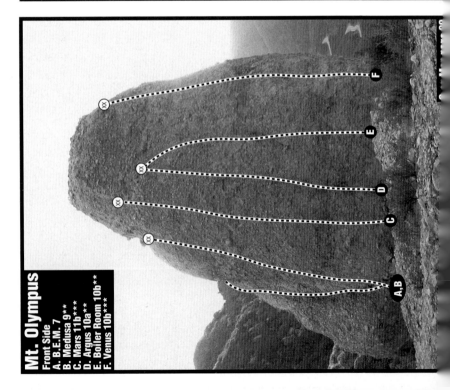

Mt. Olympus
Front Side
A. B.E.M. 7
B. Medusa 9**
C. Mars 11b***
D. Argus 10a**
E. Boiler Room 10b**
F. Venus 10b***

Mount Olympus

Backcountry Crags Intro: Page 90. Several areas in the Santa Monicas feature cobbled sections of rock, but perhaps no single crag showcases this better than Mount Olympus. The routes here can be somewhat intimidating at first glance as the bolts are a little farther apart than you might be used to, and the routes look harder than the grades shown. Rest assured that on most routes many of the cobbles that look slopey from below have positive tops or hidden holds between the cobbles.

The front side routes are in the shade until late afternoon and the right side routes are in the shade in the morning.

A. B.E.M. (Booger Eatin' Moron) 7(x)

2 bolts to 2 bolt anchor. The first route on the Tower. Begin as for *Medusa*, but head left following the ramp and clip one lonely bolt on your way to the summit.
FA: Darrell Logan, Travis Loyd, 1999.

B. Medusa 9★★

5 bolts to 2 open shuts. Climb a juggy face up to and over a flake bulge before stepping over to the right and continuing up the vertical face. Enjoyable climbing.
FA: John Long, Joe Kristy, Kelly Corcorran.

C. Mars 11b★★★

5 bolts to 2 open shuts. Diagonal slightly right to left up to and over the crux bulge, before dealing with the steep cobbles above. One of the most popular routes on the wall.
FA: John Long, Joe Kristy, Kelly Corcorran.

D. Argus 10a★★

5 bolts to shared 2 open shuts. Stem up the groove passing 3 bolts followed by steep moves on big cobbles.
FA: John Long, Joe Kristy, Kelly Corcorran.

E. Boiler Room 10b★★(r)

4 bolts to shared 2 open shuts. Looks much harder than it is as the route is filled with juggy holds.
FA: Darrell Logan, Travis Loyd, 1999.

F. Venus 10b★★★

4 bolts to 2 open shuts. Climb up the right prow. A bouldery start leads to easier climbing and a final bulge made easier by hidden jugs. ➤ Photo this page.
FA: John Long, Joe Kristy, Kelly Corcorran.

The following four routes start out of the gully on the right side of the tower. There are bolted belay stations in the gully below each route. For *Pluto*, the belay anchor is on the same face just left of the route's start.

G. Pluto 12b★

5 bolts to 2 open shuts. Climb straight up to a big cobble before climbing to the right and over a small bulge. Continue up the vertical headwall to the anchors. Somewhat loose still.
FA: John Long, Joe Kristy, Kelly Corcorran.

H. Up And Over Red 11a★★★

8 bolts to 2 Metolius rap hangers. A great introduction to the harder routes to the right. 5.10 moves up the slightly overhanging wall lead to a slight reprieve as the angle lessens before the anchors.
FA: Darrell Logan, Travis Loyd, 2000.

I. Hercules 11c★★★★

10 bolts to shared 2 open shuts. Stem across to the first bolt and then climb over instant exposure exiting from Hercules' Cave. From here fight the pump as you crank past sustained moves on the long steep wall. Some funky clips, but well protected. Easily the best route on the tower.
FA: John Long, Joe Kristy, Kelly Corcorran.

J. Incoming 11d★★

10 bolts to shared 2 open shuts. This route starts 20 feet down the gully from *Hercules*. Climb up to and then pass the cave on the right side.
FA: Darrell Logan, Travis Loyd, 2000.

Matt Callender on **Venus** 10b★★★.

Paleface
A. Project
B. Paleface 10d***

Top Hat

approach

Crag Map page 90

Jamie Hays on **Lush Life** 10a**

Paleface

Backcountry Crags Intro: Page 90. A large wall that has potential for several more routes from 5.6 to 5.12. The rock quality is good and the routes are in the shade all day long. Once fully developed, this wall coupled with Top Hat should offer a great little mini-area.

A. Project
Near the left edge of the face is this line with a single bolt up high and anchors above.

B. Paleface 10d***
7 bolts to 2 open shuts. The first route established on the wall. Start climbing ten feet left of the big bush. Climb the slightly less than vertical face to a high bulge crux.
FA: Louie Anderson, Paul Dusatko, 1996.

Top Hat
A. Satin Shoes 9**
B. Lush Life 10a**
C. Ascot 11a/b**
D. Tuxedo 12a**
E. High Ball 11a**
F. Star Dust 11d***
G. Preakness 11a***
H. Caviar 12b**

Crag Map page 90

Top Hat

A collection of short routes located on one of the highest points in the area. While the routes are fun, the real draw here is the view. Top Hat sits on a flat-topped plateau that offers comfortable lounging and 360 degree views. On a breezy day you can see all of the local islands from Catalina to the south all the way to the Channel Islands farther north. The routes only see shade in the early morning, and are described right to left as they are approached.

All routes at Top Hat were equipped by John Long, Joe Kristy, Ben Banks and Kelly Corcorran in late 2001 and early 2002.

A. Satin Shoes 9**(r)

bolts to shared 2 open shuts. Climbs the steep slab on the right edge of the formation, passing an obvious hole near the top. Slightly run out at the top.

B. Lush Life 10a**

bolts to shared 2 open shuts. Climbs the face just left of Satin Shoes and just right of the arete to a shared anchor with that route. ➤ Photo facing page.

C. Ascot 11a/b**

3 bolts to an open shut and biner anchor. Climbs the left side of the arete via an overhanging, bouldery sequence.

D. Tuxedo 12a**

3 bolts to anchor bolts just over the lip. Vertical face just left of Ascot and right of the dihedral. The climbing is harder than it looks.

E. High Ball 11a**

4 bolts to a double open shut and biner anchor. Climbs the arete just left of the dihedral. A difficult start leads to sustained 5.10 climbing.

F. Star Dust 11d***

5 bolts to a double open shut and biner anchor. Steep, reachy moves up bulging terrain lead to a thin finish. Good to the last move.

G. Preakness 11a***

4 bolts to a shared double open shut and biner anchor. Fun edge climbing on steep rock. Very enjoyable and popular.

H. Caviar 12b**

4 bolts to a shared double open shut and biner anchor. Starts in the shallow gash left of Preakness. 20 feet of bleak sidepulls and grim pinches is followed by face climbing slightly to the right. Shares the last bolt and anchors of Preakness.

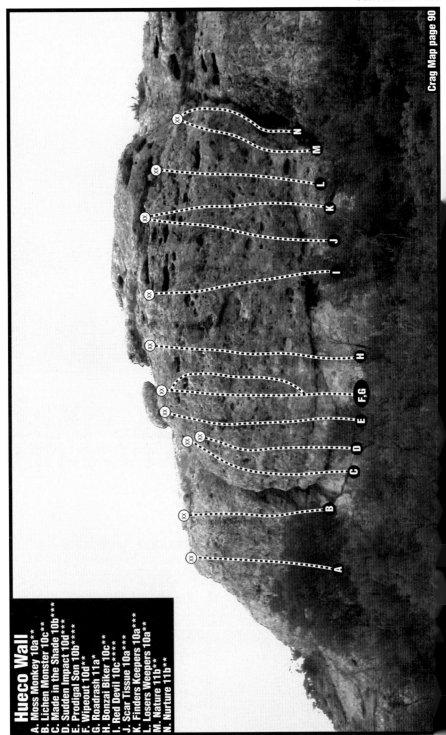

Crag Map page 90

Hueco Wall

A. Moss Monkey 10a**
B. Lichen Monster 10c**
C. Made in the Shade 10b***
D. Sudden Impact 10d***
E. Prodigal Son 10b****
F. Wipeout 10d**
G. Roadrash 11a*
H. Bonzai Biker 10c**
I. Red Devil 10c****
J. Scar Tissue 10a***
K. Finders Keepers 10a***
L. Losers Weepers 10a**
M. Nature 11b**
N. Nurture 11b**

Hueco Wall

Backcountry Crags Intro: Page 90. This moderate crag is perfect for the 5.10 climber, as almost all of its routes fall into this rating. The climbing is made up primarily of deep pockets and huecos on a vertical to slightly overhung pair of formations. The fact that the walls are in the shade for the majority of the day, makes the Hueco Wall the ideal summer option for Backbone Area climbers. The routes on this wall make perfect warm-ups for those continuing on to the more difficult climbing found at Boney Bluff.

The first two routes listed are located on the left formation and are in the shade until late afternoon.

A. Moss Monkey 10a**
3 bolts to 2 open shuts. Begin just right of a huge, oval hueco and climb the heavily pocketed face.
FA: Louie Anderson, 2001.

B. Lichen Monster 10c**
4 bolts to 2 open shuts. Starts on the right arete and traverses up and left.
FA: Louie Anderson, 2001.

The remaining routes are located on the main formation and are in the shade until mid afternoon.

C. Made in the Shade 10b***
5 bolts to 2 open shuts. This route begins in a shallow left facing corner. Climb up to and past the big hueco.
FA: Louie Anderson, 2001.

D. Sudden Impact 10d***
5 bolts to 2 open shuts. Climb over a small roof and continue up the pocketed face above, veering slightly left for the whole route.
FA: Louie Anderson, 2001.

E. Prodigal Son 10b****
6 bolts to 2 open shuts. The best route on the wall. After turning two small roofs low, follow the black streak to the top of the wall.
FA: Louie Anderson, 2001.

F. Wipeout 10d**
5 bolts to shared 2 open shuts. Starts five feet right of *Prodigal Son* and climbs the lighter colored stripe of rock.
FA: Louie Anderson, 2001.

G. Roadrash 11a*
6 bolts to shared 2 open shuts. Begin as for *Wipeout*, but after clipping its 1st bolt climb up and right following big huecos to a high bulge. Go left at the top to *Wipeout's* anchors.
FA: Louie Anderson, 2001.

H. Bonzai Biker 10c**
5 bolts to 2 open shuts. Climb straight up to a pair of basketball sized huecos and continue up the face above. Go right at the top.
FA: Louie Anderson, 2001.

I. Red Devil 10c****
5 bolts to 2 open shuts. Another great route that starts just right of a huge cobble. Climb up and left over the cobble and follow the line of bolts up the steep face.
FA: Louie Anderson, 2001.

J. Scar Tissue 10a***
5 bolts to shared 2 open shuts. Climbs the heavily huecoed face starting off the upper ledge.
FA: Louie Anderson, 2001.

K. Finders Keepers 10a***
5 bolts to shared 2 open shuts. Start climbing eight feet right of *Scar Tissue*. A great route that trends slightly right before going back left after the last bolt to the anchors of *Scar Tissue*.
FA: Louie Anderson, 2001.

L. Losers Weepers 10a**
3 bolts to 2 open shuts. Begins at a long, oval hueco and climbs past a series of huge huecos.
FA: Matt Hulet, 2001.

M. Nature 11b**
3 bolts to shared 2 open shuts. This route starts off the fern covered ledge and climbs up an ever steepening face.
FA: Daniel Drazin, 2001.

N. Nurture 11b**
3 bolts to shared 2 open shuts. Starts just right of *Nature* and climbs the right edge of the face past a powerful boulder problem crux. Go left at the top to the anchors of *Nature*.
FA: Daniel Drazin, 2001.

See Page 107 Mike Nash sticking the dyno on **Skinny White Boy** 12d***. ©*Perri Nguyen Photo.*

Boney Bluff

This small cliffband lies hidden behind the Boney Mountains, whose serrated ridgeline led to the nickname for the area—The Backbone. The Bluff is very atypical of the Santa Monicas' abundant climbing options. Although vaguely similar to some of the climbing found at Malibu Creek State Park, the Bluff has a character all its own. The routes are short (between 30 and 50 feet long) and steep (between 5 and 90 degrees past vertical). Powerful pocket climbing is the norm here on rock that can be best compared to that found at Queen Creek Canyon, outside of Superior, Arizona (home of the annual Phoenix Bouldering Contest)—without the razor sharp features.

Boney Bluff Details
Elevation: 2,900 ft.
Exposure: Mostly shady.
Sport Climbs: 39 routes, 10b to 13d.
Bouldering: 7 problems V4 to V9
Drive From Hwy 101: 20 minutes.
Drive From Hwy 1: 15 minutes
Approach: 60 to 85 minute hike.

From the beginning of the development at the Bluff, the vision was to create a "training" crag, where a relatively strong climber would feasibly be able to work any of the routes on the lead. This is achieved due to the fact that the bolts are never more than a body length apart and all of the routes can easily be "dogged." This would allow a 5.11 climber to work 5.12 routes on the lead, and a 5.12 climber to work 5.13 routes on the lead. There are also a staggering number of link-ups (only the most popular are shown) at the Bluff, allowing climbers to use moves that they have already worked on one route, to benefit them toward a redpoint of another. Add to this a 180-degree ocean view, shade almost all day long and amazing bouldering and you get a power crag that beats anything else in Southern California.

The Approach: Map page 50. This area can be approached from either the Mishe Mokwa or the Backbone Trailhead.

From the Backbone Trailhead (see page 90 for driving information): Follow the steep fire road that leaves from the north end of the parking area. At 0.3 miles you will reach a junction with the Mishe Mokwa connector trail on your right. Continue on the main fire road to Sandstone Peak. From here either continue on the fire road down to your right (if riding bikes) or head down a shortcut footpath straight ahead from the uphill approach fire road. This footpath will join up with the main fire road after a few minutes, but will save at least five minutes of hiking time. Shortly after rejoining the fire road you will encounter a sharp left hand turn in the road leading to a steep descent section, where the road is covered with chain-link fencing for improved traction. After crossing the chain-link section of road, you will pass an obvious cobbled tower on your left (Mount Olympus). Continue on the fire road, passing several more formations until you reach a junction with another fire road (on your left). You will see a pair of water tanks on the hillside up and left. Follow the right hand road (leading downhill) until it flattens out just before you reach an obvious dry creekbed. Turn left here and cross another creekbed (actually a continuation of the one that was ahead of you). Just after the creekbed a faint trail (the

Backbone Trail) leaves on your left. Follow this trail as it parallels the creekbed. After about 10 minutes you will cross the creekbed again and reach a junction with the Tri-Peaks trail. Continue on the left trail passing a sign informing you that you are now "Entering State Park Property." Shortly after passing this sign (and before the trail heads downhill again) leave the main trail and follow a faint trail on your right leading up to the obvious formation on the hill to your right that is Boney Bluff. Approximately 60-80 minutes hiking time.

From the Mishe Mokwa Trailhead (see page ?? for driving information): From the parking area, follow the trail uphill. At 0.6 miles you will reach a junction with the Backbone connector trail, which cuts back uphill on your left. Continue on the Mishe Mokwa trail as it drops into and skirts the valley below. After approximately 1.9 miles of hiking you will reach the Split Rock Picnic Area. Continue on the Mishe Mokwa trail past this picnic area passing several unclimbed rock formations on both your left and right sides. Roughly 15 minutes after passing the picnic area the trail will loop back uphill to the left and you will see a heavily huecoed formation straight ahead (see photo page 100). This is the Hueco Wall. Continue hiking on the trail (past the Hueco Wall) until you reach an obvious dry creekbed. Just after this creekbed a fire road will continue in front of you up the hill. Turn right here and cross another creekbed (actually a continuation of the one you just crossed). Just after the creekbed a faint trail (the Backbone Trail) leaves on your left. Follow this trail as it parallels the creekbed. After about 10 minutes you will cross the creekbed again and reach a junction with the Tri-Peaks trail. Continue on the left trail passing a sign informing you that you are now "Entering State Park Property." Shortly after passing this sign (and before the trail heads downhill again) leave the main trail and follow a faint trail on your right leading up to the obvious formation on the hill to your right that is Boney Bluff. Approximately 65-85 minutes hiking time.

Main Wall

This is one of the most impressive pieces of rock in Southern California (from a sport climbing perspective). When seen from the approach at the right end of the wall, it looks like a breaking wave as it gets steeper and steeper the further you go toward the left end of the wall. The wall is littered with pockets of all shapes, sizes and depths. In fact out of all of the routes found here there are only 20 or so holds that aren't pockets. Most of the harder routes tend to follow lines of smaller pockets and can be somewhat fingery, with at least one mono move on the majority of them.

Other than the open project at the far left of the developed section of cliff and the steep faces to its left, there is still room for several moderate routes up to sixty feet tall at the right end of the crag on either side of *Funky Pump* and *Europa*. There is also considerable potential for new boulder problems along the base of the wall (beginning with the sit starts to most of the lead routes).

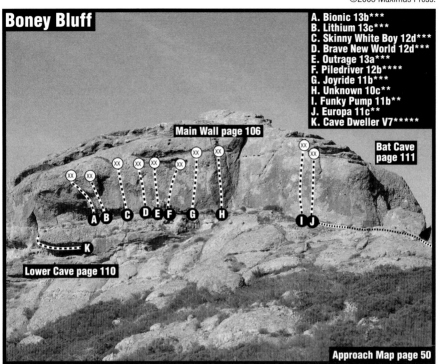

Boney Bluff

A. Bionic 13b***
B. Lithium 13c***
C. Skinny White Boy 12d***
D. Brave New World 12d***
E. Outrage 13a***
F. Piledriver 12b****
G. Joyride 11b***
H. Unknown 10c**
I. Funky Pump 11b**
J. Europa 11c**
K. Cave Dweller V7*****

Main Wall page 106

Bat Cave
page 111

Lower Cave page 110

Approach Map page 50

Matt Callender on **Piledriver** 12b****.

See Page 109

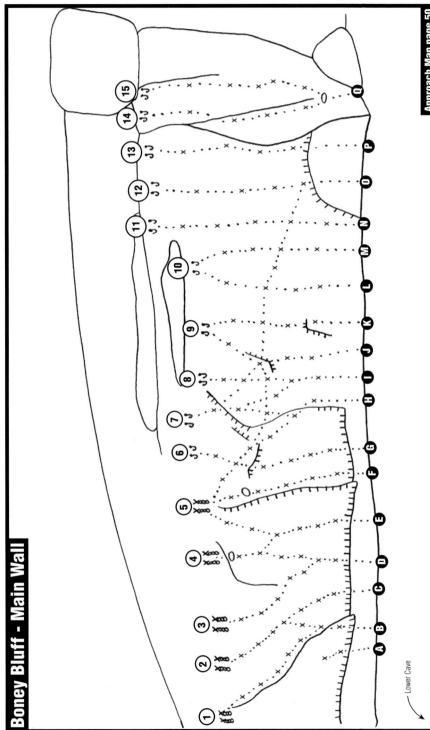

Boney Bluff - Main Wall

Approach Map page 50

Lower Cave

Boney Bluff - Main Wall

Intro: Page 103.

A. Open Project 14?

Only the first two bolts have been installed on this extremely steep face. There is quite a bit of new route potential left of this as well.

B to 1. Bionic 13b***

7 bolts to a double biner anchor. Climbs the left wall of the super steep corner, with a hard mono move.

FA: Louie Anderson, 1996.

B to 2. Biosphere 13c/d***

7 bolts to a double biner anchor. A link-up. Start on *Bionic*, but after clipping its 2nd bolt climb up and right passing one independent bolt before joining *Atmosphere* at its 4th bolt.

FA: Louie Anderson, 1996.

C to 2. Atmosphere 13d***

7 bolts to a double biner anchor. Climb up the prow before moving left onto the steep bulge. Currently the hardest route at the crag.

FA: Louie Anderson, 1997.

D to 3. Lithium 13c***

7 bolts to a double biner anchor. Begin climbing as for *Sureshot*, but after clipping its 2nd bolt climb up and left onto the steep left headwall. ➤ Photo page 93.

FA: Louie Anderson, 1997.

D to 4. Sureshot 13a***

6 bolts to a double biner anchor. The first route bolted at the crag. After pulling the initial bulge, climb up the center of the face above.

FA: Louie Anderson, 1995.

E to 4. Garbage 13a**

6 bolts to a double biner anchor. This route starts eight feet right of *Sureshot* and climbs past 4 bolts before moving left to join that route at its 5th bolt.

FA: Louie Anderson, 1996.

E to 5. Filth Pig 13b***

6 bolts to a double biner anchor. Climbs *Garbage*, but after clipping its 4th bolt move up and right passing two independent bolts before finishing at the anchors of *Skinny White Boy*. ➤ Rear cover photo.

FA: Louie Anderson, 1997.

F to 5. Skinny White Boy 12d***

5 bolts to a double biner anchor. Follows the steep dihedral with big moves between positive holds. ➤ Photo page 102.

FA: Tom Wight, 1996.

G to 5. Grunt Plus 12d**

6 bolts to a double biner anchor. A link-up. Climb *Grunt*, but at the horizontal shelf go left, clipping one independent bolt before joining *Skinny White Boy* at its last bolt.

FA: Louie Anderson, 1996.

G to 6. Grunt 12c***

6 bolts to 2 open shuts. Starts eight feet right of *Skinny White Boy* at a pair of large pockets. Climb straight up the steepening orange face, passing a horizontal shelf at 2/3 height.

FA: Louie Anderson, 1995.

H to 5. Chubby 12d**

7 bolts to a double biner anchor. A link-up. Start on *Brave New World*, but after clipping that route's 2nd bolt move up and left, following the horizontal shelf to the anchors of *Skinny White Boy.*

FA: Louie Anderson, 1996.

H to 6. Brave New Grunt 12c/d**

6 bolts to 2 open shuts. A link-up. Climb *Chubby*, but finish at the anchors of *Grunt.*

FA: Louie Anderson, 1996.

H to 7. Brave New World 12d***

5 bolts to 2 open shuts. This route begins at a small dihedral at the base of the wall. Climb up to and over the high bulge before going left to the anchors.

FA: Louie Anderson, 1996.

I to 5. Lurker 13a/b**

9 bolts to a double biner anchor. A link-up. Start on *Outrage*, but after clipping that route's 2nd bolt climb left finishing at the anchors of *Skinny White Boy.*

FA: Louie Anderson, 1996.

I to 6. Outrageous New Grunt 13a/b**

8 bolts to 2 open shuts. A link-up. Climb *Lurker*, but finish at the anchors of *Grunt.*

FA: Louie Anderson, 1996.

I to 7. Out of this World 13a**

5 bolts to 2 open shuts. A link-up. Climb *Lurker*, but finish at the anchors of *Brave New World.*

FA: Louie Anderson, 1996.

I to 8. Outrage 13a***

5 bolts to 2 open shuts. Begin climbing off a flat rock, at 2 large pockets. Climb straight up the 30 degree overhung face on small pockets.

FA: Louie Anderson, 1995.

I to 9. Eraserhead 12c***

5 bolts to 2 open shuts. A link-up. Start on *Outrage*, but after clipping that route's 3rd bolt go right, following the flat shelf and finish on *Piledriver.*

FA: Louie Anderson, 1996.

Continued next page.

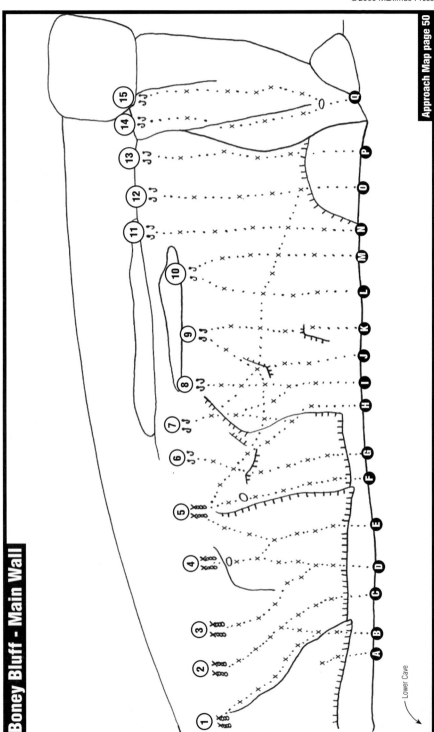

Boney Bluff - Main Wall

Approach Map page 50

Lower Cave

Boney Bluff - Main Wall

Intro: Page 103.

J to 5. Ramrod 13a**

10 bolts to a double biner anchor. A link-up. Follow *Piledriver* to its 2nd bolt before traversing left to finish at the anchors of *Skinny White Boy*.
FA: Louie Anderson, 1996.

J to 6. Gruntpile 12d**

9 bolts to 2 open shuts. A link-up. Climb *Ramrod*, but finish at the anchors of *Grunt*.
FA: Louie Anderson, 1996.

J to 7. Pile of Pockets 12d**

5 bolts to 2 open shuts. A link-up. Climb *Ramrod*, but finish at the anchors of *Brave New World*.
FA: Louie Anderson, 1996.

J to 8. Pile of Rage 13a***

5 bolts to 2 open shuts. A link-up. Begin on *Piledriver*, but after clipping that route's 2nd bolt climb up and left to finish on *Outrage*.
FA: Louie Anderson, 1996.

J to 9. Piledriver 12b****

4 bolt to 2 open shuts. Starts off the same flat rock as *Outrage*, just to the right of that route. Start off the two small pockets just below the first bolt. A series of large pockets lead to a flat shelf. From here climb up and right on mainly positive holds. Very popular. ➤ Photo page 105.
FA: Louie Anderson, 1996.

K to 9. Parallel Universe 11c**

4 bolts to 2 open shuts. Just to the right of the flat rock is a right facing flake. Climb this until it ends and continue on big pockets, finishing at the anchors of *Piledriver*.
FA: Scott Sanchez, 1996.

L to 10. Brain Stew 12b/c**

4 bolts to 2 open shuts. Start on the ground between the big boulder and the wall. Climb straight up the lighter colored face. After clipping the 4th bolt traverse right to shared anchors with *Headrush*.
FA: Louie Anderson, 1996.

M to 10. Headrush 11d**

4 bolts to 2 open shuts. Begin climbing off the ground just to the right of the big boulder. Climbs the 20 degree overhanging face. You might want to preclip the first bolt from the boulder.
FA: Louie Anderson, 1996.

N to 9. Joy Stew 12b/c**

7 bolts to 2 open shuts. A link-up. Start as for *Joyride*, but after clipping that route's 2nd bolt traverse left, finishing at the anchors of *Piledriver*.
FA: Louie Anderson, 1996.

N to 10. Joy Rush 12a**

4 bolts to 2 open shuts. A link-up. Start as for *Joyride*, but after clipping that route's 2nd bolt climb up and left to join *Headrush* at its 3rd bolt.
FA: Bruce Anderson, 1995.

N to 11. Joyride 11b***

5 bolts to 2 open shuts. The standard warm-up route on the wall. Starts just right of *Headrush* and climbs through several small bulges on mainly positive holds.
FA: Louie Anderson, 1996.

O to 5. The Long Haul 13c****

12 bolts to a double biner anchor. This route is the mother of all Bluff link-ups. Begin climbing on *The Prophet* and traverse left all the way to the anchors of *Skinny White Boy*, passing many cruxes along the way.
FA: Louie Anderson, 1996.

O to 12. The Prophet 11d**

4 bolts to 2 open shuts. Starts off a flat boulder and climbs through a severe bulge before finishing on gentler terrain.
FA: Pierre Daigle, 1996.

P to 13. The Alchemist 11b**

4 bolts to 2 open shuts. Climbs the sharp, right arete to a high bulge.
FA: Pierre Daigle, 1996.

The next two routes are located on the narrow left face of a large corner, just around to the right from *The Alchemist*.

Q to 14. Unknown 10c**

4 bolts to 2 open shuts. Begins at a hueco and climbs straight up the wall on positive holds.

Q to 15. Unknown 10b*

5 bolts to 2 open shuts. This route starts at the same place as the last route, but climbs up and right, staying just left of the deep groove until the end of the route.

The next two routes are found about sixty feet right of the corner, on the taller portion of the wall.

R. Funky Pump 11b**

5 bolts to 2 open shuts. Starts just above a huge hole in the rock. Climb past flakes and big pockets to a high crux.
FA: Louie Anderson, 1996.

S. Europa 11c**

5 bolts to 2 open shuts. Begin five feet right of *Funky Pump* and climb the blanker face to another high crux.
FA: Louie Anderson, 1996.

T. Abandoned Project

On the right corner of the formation, there are chain anchors above an unclimbed steep bulge.

Annie McMillan nearing the end of **Cave Dweller** V7*****.

Lower Cave

Boney Bluff Intro: Page 103. If only the floor of this shallow cave extended another twenty feet to allow for safe falls from the lip, it would be one of the best bouldering venues around. Unfortunately it doesn't and so the main offering of the Lower Cave is the incredible fifty-foot long *Cave Dweller* traverse. The V7 rating is assuming that all of the largest holds are used, and as such there are unlimited options for eliminates along the traverse itself as well as for short vertical problems to various jugs in the ceiling of the cave. Very little effort has been put into establishing these other problems and for a committed boulderer, many days could be spent doing nothing else at almost any grade. The bolted roof routes follow some of the more obvious would-be boulder problems and are quite difficult despite their length.

A. Fringe Dweller V4***
Sit start ten feet right of the start of the cave and climb the finish of *Cave Dweller*.

B. Remora 13c*
3 bolts to a double biner anchor. Start twenty feet right of the start of the cave and climb out the horizontal roof.
FA: Louie Anderson, 1997.

C. Undertow 13c*
4 bolts to a double biner anchor. This route begins fifteen feet right of *Remora* and also climbs the roof, joining *Remora* at its 2nd bolt.
FA: Louie Anderson, 1997.

D. Cave Dweller V7*****
Sit start and traverse the cave from right to left topping ou at the far left of the cave. ➤ Photo this page.

E. Riptide 13d***
4 bolts to a double biner anchor. A link-up. Climb the *Cave Dweller* traverse and finish on *Undertow*.
FA: Louie Anderson, 1997.

Bat Cave

Approach Map page 50

Bat Cave

First found during a break between redpoint burns by Grahm Doe and Scott Sanchez, this cave is located around to the right from the main wall and up on an almost hidden ledge. It offers four quality, steep problems climbing out an extremely steep swell/roof. There is potential for additional problems here, as well as on the several steep boulders and faces at this end of the formation.

All problems listed have sit starts.

A. Bloodsucker V8**

Starts near the right side of the deepest section of cave with the right hand in a big pocket on the lip. Climb straight out the scoop above, finishing to the left.

B. Boy Wonder V9***

Begin climbing five feet right of *Bloodsucker,* with your left hand in a good 4-finger pocket. Features a long pull to 2-finger pocket off a right hand mono. Finishes up and left.

C. The Joker V7***

This problem starts at the beginning of the rock shelf base big pockets. Climb through the roof, staying left of the big hueco.

D. Flying Blind V7***

Start as for *The Joker,* but climb the roof, passing directly over the big hueco and finishing up and right.

This next problem is located below and about 100 feet to the right of the Bat Cave, on a solitary boulder located between two larger boulders/formations.

E. The Fin V4***

Sit start and climb the sharp right arete to the top, staying on the overhanging side of the boulder.

The Fin

See Page 116

Aron Couzens on the powerful lower crux of **Conspiracy** 12a****.

The Lookout

A very convenient crag, featuring good rock and a short approach. Originally only the steep east face was developed, but now that the other routes have been bolted this wonderful little crag offers something for everyone. Rock quality is comparable to the White Wall at Echo Cliffs.

The Lookout Details

Elevation: 2,100 ft.
Exposure: Varied, sun and shade.
Sport Climbs: 15 routes, 10a to 13c.
Drive From the 101: 15 minutes.
Drive From Hwy 1: 15 minutes
Approach: 10 to 15 minute hike.

See Page 116

Doniel Drazin on **Eye to the Sky** 11b****.

Adapted from the U.S.G.S 1:24,000 Triunfo Pass Quadrangle.

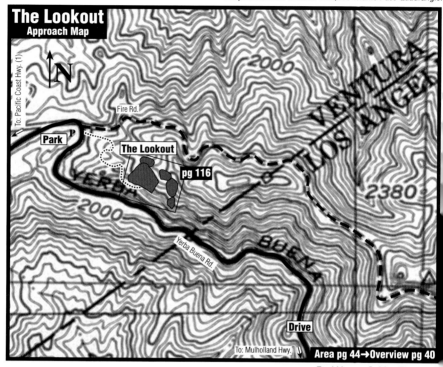

Traci Marx on **Golden Eye** 11a**

The Approach: This area can be approached from either the Ventura Freeway (101) or the Pacific Coast Highway (1).

Ventura Freeway (101): Exit the freeway at the Westlake Blvd. (Hwy 23) exit and head south (towards the ocean). You will pass through a couple of traffic signals before coming to a stop sign at Potrero Rd. (mile 1.6 from the 101). Continue through this stop sign, passing a large rock formation on your right until you reach another stop sign at Carlisle Canyon Rd. (mile 2.7). Drive straight through this intersection and follow the road as it winds up through the hills. At mile 4.7 you will merge with Mulholland Dr., which comes in from your left. Continue on through this intersection until you reach a stop sign (mile 6.4), with Mulholland Dr. continuing on your right. Turn here and then turn right again onto Little Sycamore Canyon Rd. (mile 6.7). This road will wind through the hills, changing its name to Yerba Buena Rd. At mile 8.5 you will reach a small development of homes at a sharp left turn in the road. Park in the large dirt turnout on your left at the bend in the road

Pacific Coast Highway (1): From the Pacific Coast Hwy. (1), head inland on Yerba Buena Rd. (located adjacent to Neptune's Net restaurant). Head up into the hills, passing a junction with Cortharin Rd. at 2.9 miles. At 3.8 miles you will pass the Circle X Ranger Station on your right and then the Backbone Trailhead at mile 4.8. From here continue on Yerba Buena Road to mile 12.1, where a small development of homes will be encountered on your left at a sharp right turn in the road. Park in the large dirt turnout on your right, at the bend in the road.

Decker Rd. (23): You can also leave Pacific Coast Hwy. (1) and head inland on Decker Rd. (23 North). Follow this road for 4.8 miles until you reach a stop sign at Mulholland Dr., which comes in from your left. Turn left here and continue to a right turn onto Little Sycamore Canyon Rd. (mile 5.1 from Pacific Coast Hwy.). This road will wind through the hills, changing name to Yerba Buena Rd. before reaching a small development of homes at a sharp left turn in the road (mile 6.9). This is the parking area for The Lookout. Park in the large dirt turnout on your left at the bend in the road

From the parking area, cross the road and go through a break in the bushes, to the right of the driveway leading up to the fire road. A faint trail leads uphill and slightly to the right, heading more or less toward the large boulder on the hill above you. Once you reach the boulder, a trail will leave the open area and head through a break in the bushes on your right. Follow this, dropping down into a recessed area before climbing back out on the far side. Shortly after coming up from the recess you will intersect with a recently constructed extension of the Backbone Trail. Turn right here and follow the trail as it winds around the opposite side of the hill. Just before reaching the formation, a steep trail leaves the Backbone Trail heading down and right. Follow this trail around to the front of the formation and the routes.

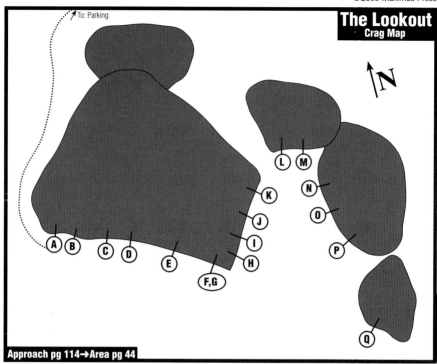

The Lookout
Intro: Page 113.

A. Spy Games 10b★★
3 bolts to 2 shared open shuts. Climbs the far left bolt line up slightly overhung rock to a huge cobble.
FA: Louie Anderson, 2002.

B. Espionage 10c★★★
3 bolts to 2 shared open shuts. An easy start leads to steep edges and the same finishing move as *Spy Games.*
FA: Louie Anderson, 2002.

C. Double Agent 10a★★★★
4 bolts to 2 shared open shuts. Start just right of *Espionage* and climb up and right to a rest below the final bulge.
FA: Louie Anderson, 2002.

D. Hidden Agenda 11b★★★
4 bolts to 2 shared open shuts. Climb the shallow center prow on thin, technical moves to finish on the final bulge of *Double Agent.*
FA: Louie Anderson, 2002.

E. Eye to the Sky 11b★★★★
5 bolts to 2 shared open shuts. Climbs straight up to and through the steep dihedral at the top of the wall.
➤ Photo pages 113, 228.
FA: Louie Anderson, 2002.

F. Informer 11c★★★★
6 bolts to 2 shared open shuts. A link-up. Start up the first four bolts of *Incognito,* then traverse left to join *Eye to the Sky* at its 4th bolt.
FA: Doniel Drazin, 2002.

G. Incognito 11c★★★★★
6 bolts to 2 open shuts. Follow the rightmost bolt line using the arete itself towards the top. A sustained and popular route.
FA: Doniel Drazin, 2002.

H. Conspiracy 12a★★★★
5 bolts to 2 open shuts. Pre-clip the first bolt and climb the arete. A hard deadpoint low leads to sustained climbing.
➤ Photo pages 14, 112.
FA: Louie Anderson, 1995.

I. Big Brother 13c/d★★★
3 bolts to 2 shared open shuts. Start off the "patio" and climb the center of the face using many thin edges and crimps. A very sustained route and the hardest at the crag.
FA: Louie Anderson, 1995.

J. Contact 13a★★★
3 bolts to 2 shared open shuts. Climb the face to the right of *Big Brother,* starting matched on the big flake, and finishing at the same anchors as that route.
FA: Louie Anderson, 1995.

The Lookout
A. Spy Games 10b**
C. Double Agent 10a****
E. Eye to th Sky 11b****
G. Incognito 11c*****
P. Top Secret 11d**
Q. Golden Eye 11a**

Approach

:. Protocol 11a*

bolts to 2 open shuts. The original warm up route at the
ag. Now that the front side has been developed, this
ute may not be worth bothering with.
: Louie Anderson, 1995.

he following routes are located on the
ces opposite the east face.

. Octopussy 10a**

bolts to 2 open shuts. Begin climbing just right of the
ete and move up to the flat shelf. Travese up and left at
e top.
Doniel Drazin, 2003.

1. Pussy Galore 10d**

bolts to 2 open shuts. Start off the big knob and climb
rough the scoop with big moves to huge, flat cobbles.
Doniel Drazin, 2003.

1. L.A. Confidential 10d***

bolts to 2 open shuts. Starting off pinches, climb up and
ghtly right over 2 small bulges via fun, sometimes long
oves.
Doniel Drazin, 2002.

O. Central Intelligence 10c*

3 bolts to 2 shared open shuts. Follows the right
diagonalling ramp and seam past 2 bolts to join *Top
Secret* at its last bolt.
FA: Doniel Drazin, 2002.

P. Top Secret 11d**

3 bolts to 2 shared open shuts. Preclip the first bolt and
climb through bouldery moves, on smallish holds.
Beware, as the second clip is difficult.
FA: Doniel Drazin, 2002.

Q. Golden Eye 11a**

4 bolts to 2 open shuts. This route starts down at the
bottom of the rightmost formation. Its base can be
reached by scrambling down a series of small boulders.
Climb up and over the bulge. ➤ Photo page 114.
FA: Doniel Drazin, 2003.

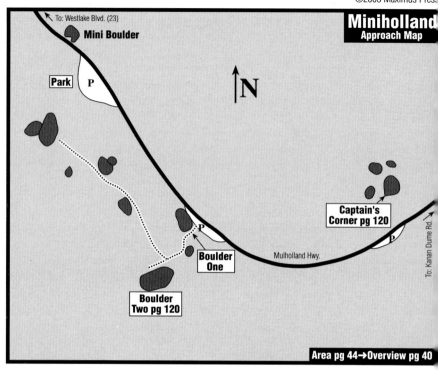

Miniholland

A great roadside bouldering area that allows for lunchtime and evening sessions for area climbers. Miniholland has seen climbing activity for many years, and with good reason. The bouldering (especially on Boulder One and Two) is top notch, and the rock quality is far above average for the area. Three separate bouldering areas

Miniholland Details

Elevation: 2,000 ft.
Exposure: Varied.
Bouldering: 50+ problems, VB to V5.
Drive From the 101: 15 minutes.
Drive From Hwy 1: 20 minutes
Approach: 1 minute.

are described here, however there are a vast number of unclimbed boulder located on the surrounding hillsides and an adventurous developer could no doubt find several gems.

The best bouldering is found on Boulder One and Two, but there has bee activity on the clusters of boulders found downhill from Boulder One, includ ing some taller and steeper problems on the largest of those boulders. There also climbing to be found on the Mini Boulder and up the road a bit at th Captain's Corner area. The latter area boasted some proud highballs, includ ing the namesake *Captain's Corner* (V5**), but they became overgrown an forgotten until a group of Los Angeles based boulderers rediscovered it i 2002.

The climbing consists primarily of pockets on good quality rock. Because of the high traffic at the area over the years, it's likely that all variations and link-ups have been climbed at the main boulders. Just about every usable feature is chalked and as such it's difficult to determine which are the original problems. Instead of making an attempt to decipher the individual problems, this guide will just suggest that most of the climbing is between V0 and V5, with some exceptions at either end of the scale. The landings are usually pretty flat and easy access with a pad can be found to most problems.

The Approach: *From the Ventura Freeway (101),* follow Westlake Blvd. (23 South) towards the ocean, until you reach Mulholland Dr. on your left at mile 4.7 (from the 101 Fwy.). Turn left here and at mile 5.6 you will see a large boulder directly off the road on your right hand side. Either park in the turnout next to the boulder or head back downhill to the large dirt turnout area.

From the Pacific Coast Highway (1), head inland on Decker Rd. (23 North). At mile 4.8 you will merge with Mulholland Dr., which comes in from your left. At an intersection located at mile 6.5 Mulholland Dr. continues on the right. Turn right here and at mile 7.4 you will see a large boulder directly off the road on your right hand side. Either park in the turnout next to the boulder or head back downhill to the large dirt turnout area.

Miniholland
Boulder One

Miniholland
Boulder Two

Approach Map page 118

Miniholland
A. Captain's Corner V5**(h)

A

Matt Callender on **Boulder Two's** clean north face.

Cave X

No directions are given to this cave as there is currently no legal access The cave and the adjacent cliffs are located on land that is part of the Conejo Open Space Conservation Area (COSCA). Currently COSCA does not allow climbing on their properties. This area has been included in the guide in the hope that access may be restored at some point in the future.

Cave X was once a hangout for the homeless and for local partiers. As such it was covered with graffiti and filled with trash when climbers first visited. The original developers spent hours cleaning the walls and removing trash of all types and sizes, including old mattresses. The rangers realize and appreciate this clean up effort, but do not condone climbing activities. In the past climbers have been asked to leave, but to date no one has been ticketed since the cave has a history of climbing activity.

Doniel Drazin on **Bump and Grind** 13b****.

Cave X

A. Retro Funk 11c*
3 bolts to 2 open shuts. Climb up and left to the dihedral, and follow this to the anchors.

B. Down and Out 13a**
5 bolts to a double biner anchor. Clip the first bolt of *Retro Funk* and then continue up the steep face above, following a series of thin pockets to a high bulge crux.

C. Interview With a Vampire 11c
3 bolts to 2 open shuts. This route starts just around the corner to the right of *Down and Out*. Climb the right side of the arete following the diagonalling seam. The route traverses right at the top to the anchors of *Trauma*.

D. Trauma 12d**
3 bolts to 2 open shuts. A very thin route that climbs to the solitary pocket high on the route.

E. Code Blue 12b***
3 bolts to a double chain anchor. A very clean route that follows a line of crimps and sidepulls up nice quality limestone.

F. Triple Bypass 11b**
3 bolts to 2 open shuts. Climbs the overhanging corner deep in the cave. Can be somewhat dark on all but the brightest of days.

G. Open Project
Partially bolted. Follows the left diagonalling line to finish at the anchors of *Triple Bypass*.

H. Open Project
Partially bolted. This route climbs up to and then follows the very overhung crack to chain anchors.

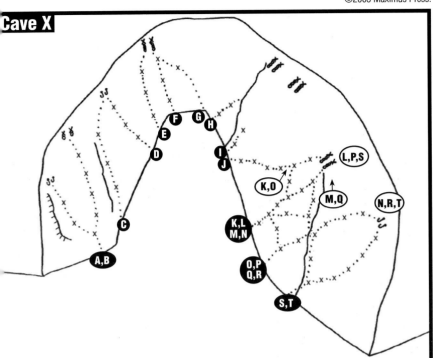

Cave X

. Open Project

artially bolted. Only two bolts so far on this 45 degree
verhung face, ending at chain anchors.

. Hummer 13c***

bolts to a double chain anchor. Begin climbing a few
et right of the *Open Project* and traverse up and right
imbing through a difficult pocket sequence.

. Lurch 13c***

bolts to a double chain anchor. Start climbing directly
elow the huge cobble and under a small roof. Climb up
the 4th bolt before moving left to join and finish on
ummer.

. Bump and Grind 13b****

bolts to a double chain anchor. Start as for *Lurch,* but
ntinue climbing straight up after clipping the 4th bolt.
Photo facing page.

. Bloodsucker 12d**

bolts to a double chain anchor. Same start as *Bump and
rind,* but after clipping the 2nd bolt move up and right.
hen you reach the crack follow it left to the anchors.

. Humble Pie 13a****

bolts to 2 open shuts. Climb *Bloodsucker,* but when you
ach the crack cross it and continue up the bolt line
ove.

O. Ballistic 13d****

8 bolts to a double chain anchor. Start climbing about 8
feet right of *Bump and Grind.* After clipping the 1st bolt
traverse left along the lip of the low roof, finishing up
Lurch.

P. Lip Service 13b***

7 bolts to a double chain anchor. Climb *Ballistic,* but
finish up *Bump and Grind.*

Q. Heartbreaker 13a**

6 bolts to a double chain anchor. Start as for *Ballistic,* but
climb straight up to the crack and follow it left to the
anchors.

R. Pacemaker 13a***

6 bolts to 2 open shuts. Climb *Heartbreaker,* but when you
reach the crack cross it and join *Humble Pie.*

S. Stinger 12d***

6 bolts to a double chain anchor. Follow the left
diagonalling crack.

T. Project

6 bolts to 2 open shuts. Start climbing as for *Stinger,* but
after clipping the 1st bolt move right around the corner and
follow the steep line of bolts. This project would surely
result in a 5.14, however it lies on the more visible mouth
of the cave and the equipper stopped climbing here before
it could be redpointed.

See Page 151

Diana Jew on **The Drifter** 12a***** at Malibu Creek. ©*Perri Nguyen Phot*

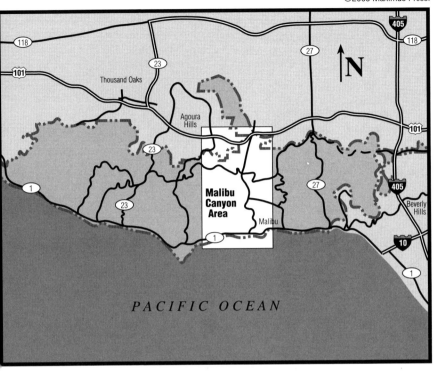

CHAPTER 3

MALIBU CANYON

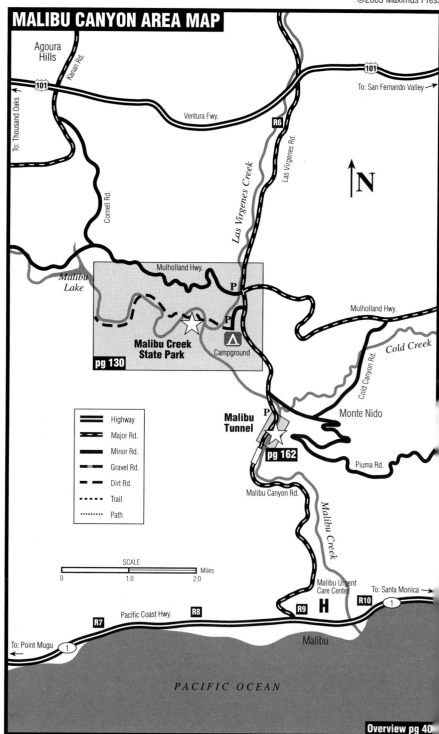

MALIBU CANYON AREA MAP

Agoura Hills

Kanan Rd.

101

Ventura Fwy.

To: San Fernando Valley →

To: Thousand Oaks →

R6

Las Virgenes Creek

Las Virgenes Rd.

Cornell Rd.

N

Malibu Lake

Mulholland Hwy.

P

Mulholland Hwy.

Cold Creek

P

Cold Canyon Rd.

Malibu Creek State Park

Campground

pg 130

Monte Nido

Malibu Tunnel

P

pg 162

Piuma Rd.

Malibu Canyon Rd.

Malibu Creek

Highway

Major Rd.

Minor Rd.

Gravel Rd.

Dirt Rd.

Trail

Path

SCALE

0   1.0   2.0   Miles

Malibu Urgent Care Center

To: Santa Monica →

H

R10

1

Pacific Coast Hwy.

R8

R9

To: Point Mugu

1

R7

Malibu

PACIFIC OCEAN

Overview pg 40

MALIBU CANYON AREA BASICS

Malibu Canyon is one of the more popular areas found in this guide. Developed climbing options exist in two separate areas; Malibu Creek State Park and Malibu Tunnel. While the climbing at Malibu Tunnel is primarily bouldering (with a few scattered top-ropes), its quality and accessibility to Malibu Creek State Park has warranted its inclusion.

Getting There

From the Ventura Fwy. (101) exit on Las Virgenes Rd. and head south. From the Pacific Coast Hwy. (1) head north on Malibu Canyon Rd.

Restaurants

R6. La Paz
Great mexican and seafood.
4505 Las Virgenes Rd.
☎ 818-880-8076.

R7. Beau Rivage
Mediterranean cuisine.
26025 Pacific Coast Hwy.
☎ 310-456-5733.

R8. Malibu Seafood Patio Café
Freshly caught seafood.
25653 Pacific Coast Hwy.
☎ 310-456-3430.

R9. Taverna Tony
Greek eats and sweets.
23410 Civic Center Way.
☎ 310-317-9667.

R10. Allegria Café
Everything Italian and more.
22821 Pacific Coast Hwy.
☎ 310-456-3132.

Camping

Malibu Creek State Park
Open all year, the fee is $12. Picnic tables, piped water, showers, flush toilets, pets OK, elev. 500 ft.
☎ 800-444-7275.

See Page 143

John Vitug on **Skeezer Pleaser** 11b**** at Malibu Creek.

Malibu Creek State Park

Malibu Creek State Park

Elevation: 500 ft.
Exposure: Varied, sun and shade.
Sport Climbs: 107 routes, 5.8 to 14a.
Top-roping: Bolt anchors, 5.9 to 13a.
Drive From the 101: 10 minutes.
Drive From Hwy 1: 15 minutes
Approach: 20 to 30 minute walk.

Made up of approximately 10,000 acres of wilderness area, Malibu Creek State Park is one of the more popular areas found in this guide. Initial developers of the Park realized that they were on to something good and intentionally spread rumors of poor rock quality and dangerous landings in an effort to keep others away from their playground. This actually worked for much of the 1980s and early 1990s.

Malibu Creek State Park offers an amazing amount of developed and undeveloped bouldering, and a wide variety of quality sport climbing. Those wishing to explore the boulder problems should be forewarned that few of the boulders offer flat landings. Water hazards and jumbled, rocky landings are far more prevalent. Because of this it is wise to be familiar with the difficulties of a given problem and be willing and able to reverse difficult sections. Perhaps because of the poor landings, several of the taller "highballs" are routinely top-roped instead. In recent years, some of the established top-ropes have been turned into sport climbs. Prior to continuing this trend please consider whether or not the potential sport route would be a truly valid addition to the Park's already abundant sport climbing options. A few of the routes listed in this guide are prime examples of routes that should have remained as top-ropes.

While climbing is an extremely popular endeavor in the Park we are not alone here. The area is a popular destination area for hikers, birdwatchers, mountain bikers and fishermen. Aside from these groups the area's many swimming holes attract the summertime masses looking to escape the heat. Unfortunately, many of these people have turned the popular swimming holes in particular, and the whole area to a lesser degree, into a giant trash dump. For the most part the climbing areas are kept pretty clean, but once you get away from these areas and closer to the popular hangs the amount and type of trash left behind is amazing. Please add a small trash bag to your pack and do your part to make an impact (however small) on cleaning up the park. The rangers have positioned trash cans at many prime locations so you should not have to carry your collection far before disposing of it.

Due to the quality of the fire roads and trails used to approach the main climbing areas a mountain bike can severely cut down on the approach time. When climbing at the Planet of the Apes wall your bike will be right next to you the entire time. If planning to climb elsewhere remember to bring a chain and lock to secure your bike to one of the many trees found throughout the Park. In most cases your bike will be out of your sight while climbing, so if you have an expensive bike this may not be a good option.

History: The earliest roped climbing here occurred on the conveniently located Planet of the Apes Wall and was limited to top-roping on this 60-foot tall, overhanging face. Initially the left and right fringes of the wall were the only sections to be successfully climbed to the summit. This all changed in 1994, when Jack Marshall decided that the vast center portion of the wall had gone unclimbed for long enough. Along with his partners, Marshall established many fine new top-ropes, some of them among the most popular climbs in the Park. Not to be missed routes on the Apes Wall include *Planet of the Apes* and *Monkey Sang, Monkey Do*. The base of this wall also offers an incredible bouldering traverse that is every bit as popular as its routes.

While bouldering beyond the Rock Pool, climbers' eyes must have continually been drawn to the towering walls on either side of the creekbed boulders. In 1985, local Dave Katz bolted *Kathmandu* and *Johnny Can't Lead* on a wall that was later to put the Park on the map. In 1991 another local developer, Bill Leventhal teamed up with John Mireles to add more routes to this wall, newly christened The Ghetto. Together this pair opened the eyes of local sport climbers by introducing a handful of sport climbs that were near the top of the local standard at that time. In particular, Mireles' redpoint of *Maximum Ghetto* brought the masses to the Park to see what all the talk was about. Shortly after this influx began, Eddie Yanik visited and began to envision a steep line up an extremely loose face to the right of the developed routes. Many days of cleaning later Yanik walked away with the first ascent of *Ghetto Blaster*, the best route on the wall. To this day The Ghetto's routes see dozens of ascents each weekend.

Until now published information on sport climbing in Malibu Creek State Park was limited to the two areas discussed above. As such, most climbing activity occurred at these areas and overcrowding was a common problem. With the release of this guide, information is now available for sport climbing in at least six major areas, with other available options shown on the area overview maps. This expanded information should alleviate the crowding problem and help to spread out climbers.

The more recent areas can by no means be dismissed as afterthoughts or "fill-ins." Several of the routes at these newer areas are the best of their grade in the Park and have already become quite popular, despite the lack of published information. Standouts of the newer routes include *Chopping Block, Nipple Denial Syndrome, Gorgeous, Delicious, Pocket Jones, Rolling Blackout, The Drifter* and *White Trash*. In addition to these newer areas, new routes have continued to be developed at The Ghetto. Perhaps the most newsworthy addition here is Dawn Diamond's redpoint of a difficult new link-up called, *Lateralus*. This incredibly steep new route is the first route in the Park to be given the 5.14 grade. New route activity around the corner to the right of the main Ghetto area by Tony Sartin shows that this wonderful wall is far from being climbed out.

Adapted from the U.S.G.S. 1:24,000 Malibu Beach Quadrangle

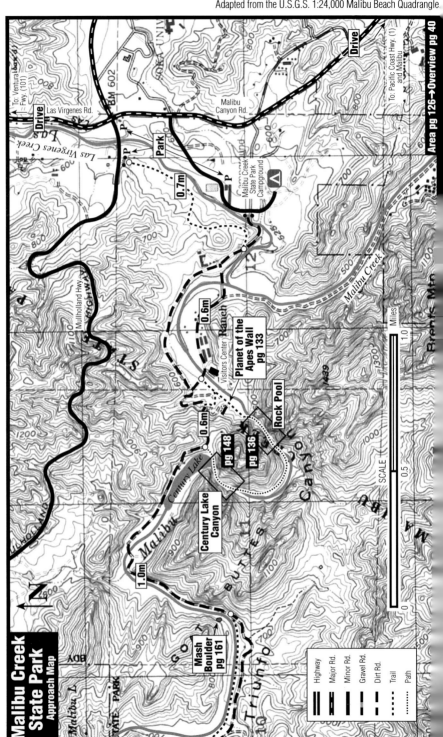

Malibu Creek State Park Approach Map

The Approach: *From the Ventura Freeway (101):* Exit the freeway at the Las Virgenes Rd. exit and head south (towards the ocean). Just after passing Mulholland Hwy. you will reach the entry gate to Malibu Creek State Park (mile 2.9 from freeway). A $2.00 entrance fee is required to park within the gate. If you would rather not pay the entrance fee, street side parking is available on Mulholland Hwy. on the west side of Las Virgenes. Park in the series of small turnouts on the Park side of Mulholland.

From the Pacific Coast Highway (1): Leave the highway at Malibu Canyon Rd. Follow this into the hills passing through a tunnel at mile 3.3, before reaching Piuma Rd. on your right. Pass Piuma and begin looking for the entry gate on your left (mile 5.6 from the Pacific Coast Hwy.). A $2.00 entrance fee is required to park within the gate. If you would rather not pay the entrance fee, streetside parking is available by continuing past the gate and turning left onto Mulholland Hwy. Park in the series of small turnouts on your left.

See Page 145

Marc Roth on **Ghetto Crossing** 13a***.

See Page 135

Fiona Visocnik on **Spider Monkey** 11b***

Planet of the Apes Wall

Malibu Creek State Park Intro: Page 128. A very popular top-roping wall that gets shade in the morning and late afternoon. There are many bolts scattered along the summit, along with some huge metal bars left over from movie riggings. A safe top-rope can be set up using these anchors and a handful of long slings or rope pieces. Be forewarned that the routes on the left side of the wall get set up early on weekends. It is common for parties of climbers to set up top-ropes on separate routes and then share their ropes with other parties. This community environment allows individual parties to get on many different climbs without having to break down and re-rig their top-ropes for every route. Please keep this in mind and share your line with others.

The routes on this wall are in the shade in the morning and late afternoon. The top of the wall can be accessed easily from the rear of the formation.

©2003 Maximus Press.

Planet of the Apes Wall
G. Planet of the Apes 11a****
K. Gorilla Warfare 12a***
N. Monkey Sang, Monkey Do 11c****

Approach Map page 130

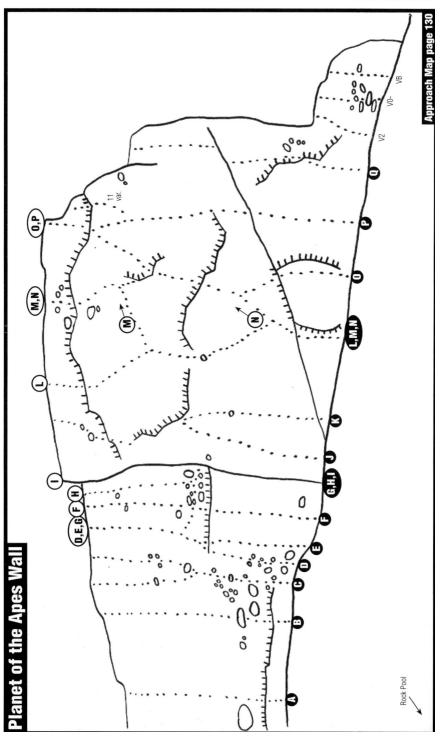

Planet of the Apes Wall

Approach Map page 130

Rock Pool

Planet of the Apes Wall

Malibu Creek Intro: Page 128.

A. Grape Ape 9(tr)

Climbs the huecoed face under the tree.

B. Christmas Pump 10a(tr)

Begin just left of the huge huecos and climb straight up on juggy pockets.

C. Shock the Monkey 10b** or 11a**(tr)

Starts just to the right of the huge huecos and climbs up to two possible finishes (both with thin cruxes). The left finish is the harder option.

D. Spiker Monkey 10c**(tr)

An easier version of the popular Spider Monkey. Start just to the right of Spider Monkey and climb diagonally up and right to join Spider Monkey as it passes the mid-height bulge on its left edge. ➤ Photo page 132.

E. Spider Monkey 11b***(tr)

A very popular line that starts up some cruxy pocket moves leading to a sloping hueco in the bulge. After crossing the bulge at its left edge enjoy easier climbing above to the top of the wall.

F. Finger Prints 11a**(tr)

Climbs the thin line of pockets 8 feet left of the corner crossing the bulge into huge huecos and pockets.

G. Planet of the Apes 11a****(tr)

The original classic on the wall. Start up the corner and upon reaching the bulge traverse left following huge features to finish up Spider Monkey. The following two routes are variation finishes to this route. ➤ Photo page 161.

H. Birthday Boy 11b**(tr)

Finish on the line of pockets 5 feet left of the crack.

I. The Crack 11b**(tr)

Finish up the crack.

J. Gorilla of My Dreams 12a***(tr)

Start this route 5 feet to the right of the corner and climb up and slightly right to the big flake at mid height. Follow this to the steeper headwall above.
FA: Jack Marshall, 1994.

K. Gorilla Warfare 12a***(tr)

7 feet to the right of Gorilla of My Dreams follow pockets directly below the big flake until you can join that route.
FA: Jack Marshall, 1994.

L. Apes of Wrath 12c/d**(tr)

The direct finish to Spank the Monkey. Climbs left from the upper portion of that route through the steep summit overhang via slopey pockets. Seldom attempted.

M. Spank the Monkey 11d***(tr)

A popular line that crosses a faint seam down low before climbing left and through the gap between roofs. From here a fun finish takes you up and right through the steep overhang.
FA: Jack Marshall, 1994.

N. Monkey Sang, Monkey Do 11c****(tr)

The second most popular route on the wall. Begin as for Spank the Monkey, but where it goes left continue up and over a small overlap before joining it again near the top of the wall.
FA: Jack Marshall, 1994.

O. Monkey Business 12b**(tr)

Climb up the right side of the scoop and then back left to join Spank the Monkey. Climb the middle of that route before leaving it at the top of the upper flake to climb a short variation right to the finishing moves of Simian Survival.
FA: Jack Marshall, 1994.

P. Simian Survival 13a**(tr)

Begin climbing where the base of the wall is slightly undercut. Climb straight up passing over the diagonal seam and very blank terrain. At roughly mid-route a rest can be found at a small roof before following a thin, left-leaning seam up through a bulge. Towards the top a left-facing flake provides easy passage to the summit bulge. This route previously used two fixed pins as directional anchors to prevent swinging falls. These pins no longer exist and the route is not as popular as it once was.
FA: Jack Marshall, 1994.

Q. Walking on the Moon 11b**(tr)

This route begins near the right edge of the main face and climbs slightly up and left to the diagonal seam. At this point traverse right on the seam until it ends at a small bulge. Climb over this and straight up, finishing on the ledge with the two big rings.

Planet of the Apes Traverse V7***

Traverses the entire wall in either direction. Towards the right end it is easier to climb up high as opposed to staying low on the undercut face. Many variations exist along the traverse.

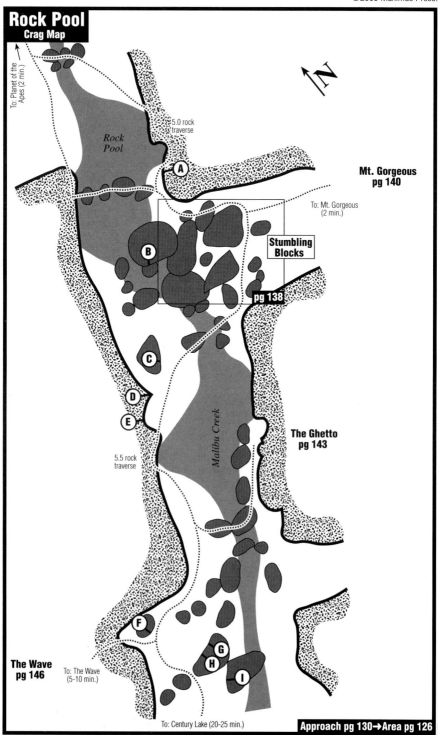

Rock Pool
Crag Map

To: Planet of the Apes (2 min.)

Rock Pool

5.0 rock traverse

A

Mt. Gorgeous
pg 140

To: Mt. Gorgeous (2 min.)

Stumbling Blocks

B

pg 138

C

D

E

Malibu Creek

The Ghetto
pg 143

5.5 rock traverse

F

The Wave
pg 146

To: The Wave (5-10 min.)

G

H

I

To: Century Lake (20-25 min.)

Rock Pool
Malibu Creek Intro: Page 128.

A. Crack Dealer 11b★★
Gear to 2.5". Climb the short flake to access the big ledge above. The route begins at the rear left corner of the ledge and climbs the overhanging corner crack.
FA: Bill Leventhal, 2001.

B. Classic Malibu Face 8★★(tr)
This route climbs the vertical face using large sloping pockets. Very popular.

C. Hot Lips 12(tr)
Prior to the development of the harder routes at the Ghetto, this top-rope was the area testpiece. Traverse up and left on flexing flakes to reach the deep hueco (stick your leg in this, knee-deep, for a great rest). Finishes with a last hard move at the top.

D. Mississippi Mud 13a/b★
4 bolts to anchors on the ledge. Climb the right arete of the cave on small edges and sidepulls before turning a bulge. From here follow large huecos to anchors on the ledge above.
FA: Eddie Yanik, 1995.

E. Project 13b?
Bolts traversing left out steepest part of cave to chain anchors.
P: Aaron Lennox.

F. Kim Chi 11d
6 bolts to a double chain anchor. Found in the creekbed immediately before heading uphill to The Wave. An old top-rope that has been turned into a short sport route (short, despite the fact that it has as many bolts as the much longer routes at The Ghetto across the canyon).
EB: Ki Bum. FA: John Long, 2002.

G. Power Beast 11c/d★(tr)
Climbs the left side of the face on small pockets and edges.

H. Celluloid Hero 11b/c★(tr)
This climbs the right side of the face with a sloping crux.

I. Lunge or Plunge 12c★★(tr)
Another old time testpiece, this problem climbs the steep bulge using small holds. The often present water landing ups the commitment level if you choose to forgo the top-rope (the original method).

Another busy day at the Rock Pool.

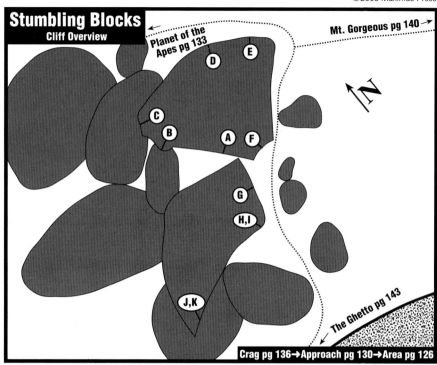

Stumbling Blocks
Cliff Overview

Planet of the Apes pg 133

Mt. Gorgeous pg 140 →

N

Crag pg 136→Approach pg 130→Area pg 126

The Ghetto pg 143

Annie McMillan on **Chopping Block** 8****.

Sandy Fee on **Letterbox** 11b/c***.

Stumbling Blocks

Malibu Creek Intro: Page 128. The first sport routes found after passing the Rock Pool, the Stumbling Blocks' routes are some of the most accessible in the Park. With routes facing all different directions, and thanks to the shade of the large adjacent trees, shady routes can be found here all day. While there are no really long routes here, just about every route is worthwhile and popular. Some of the better routes here feature short, powerful cruxes on steep terrain. The Stumbling Blocks are a popular warm-up area for climbers continuing on to either Mount Gorgeous or The Ghetto.

A. Over the Falls 11d**

6 bolts to shared open shut and biner anchor. A somewhat contrived route that starts 4 feet left of the right-hand arete. Very enjoyable steep climbing for the first four bolts leads to funky stemming off the right boulder. Leave the stem at the top of the wall in order to climb left to the anchors.
FA: Mark Fekkes, 1999.

B. Vigilante 11a***

4 bolts to shared open shut and biner anchor. Climbs the overhanging arete to the right of *Chopping Block*, ending at the anchors of *Over the Falls*.
FA: Louie Anderson, 2002.

C. Chopping Block 8****

8 bolts to 2 open shuts. Starts off the top of a pointed boulder and climbs up a very clean, less than vertical face. ➤ Photo facing page.
FA: Bill Leventhal, Matt Oliphant, Mike Draper, 1997.

D. Guerrilla Drilla 10a***

5 bolts to 2 chains. Climb an initial slabby section to a ledge. From here an ever-steepening face leads to the anchors.
FA: Bill Leventhal, Matt Oliphant, Mike Draper, 1998.

E. The Third Degree 10b***

4 bolts to 1 open shut and 1 biner. The first route bolted at the Stumbling Blocks. Step up onto the face over a small void, and climb up and left before blasting up the steep face.
FA: Bill Leventhal, Matt Oliphant, Mike Draper, 1997.

F. X-Files 10c**

4 bolts to double biner anchor. This route begins on the narrow, wedge-shaped face and climbs the left arete through a bulge. Finishes on the vertical upper face.
FA: Bill Leventhal, Matt Oliphant, Mike Draper, 1997.

G. Mr. Big 10d***

6 bolts to shared double biner anchor. Starts 10 feet left of *X-Files* (on the other boulder) and traverses diagonally up and left, eventually joining *Nipple Denial Syndrome* at its last bolt.
FA: Louie Anderson, 2002.

H. Nipple Denial Syndrome 11a/b***

5 bolts to shared double biner anchor. Start just left of the arete and climb straight up, following the line of the arete.
FA: Bill Leventhal, Matt Oliphant, Mike Draper, 1997.

I. Letterbox 11b/c***

4 bolts to 1 open shut and 1 biner. Shares the opening moves of *Nipple Denial Syndrome*. After clipping the 1st bolt climb up and left, traversing diagonally through the steep scoop. After a powerful crux, turn the lip and continue past enjoyable climbing on the face above. ➤ Photo this page.
FA: Bill Leventhal, Matt Oliphant, Mike Draper, 1997.

J. Blockbuster 11a***

5 bolts to 1 open shut and 1 biner. Begin a few feet right of the sharp arete on a large flat edge. Climb straight up to the arete and follow it to the top of the boulder.
FA: Bill Leventhal, Matt Oliphant, Mike Draper, 1998.

K. New Release 12a**

5 bolts to 1 open shut and 1 biner. A variation. Start as for *Blockbuster* and follow the same bolt line, but do not use the arete at all.
FA: Mark Fekkes, 1999.

Brandon Thau on **Delicious** 10d/11a*****.

Mount Gorgeous

Located just a few minutes uphill from the Stumbling Blocks, Mount Gorgeous offers some of the longer sport routes to be found in Malibu Creek. More of a beginner and intermediate crag, this is fast becoming one of the most popular areas in the Park. While the routes themselves are only in the shade in the morning, the base of the routes feature all day shade thanks to the canopy of mature Oak trees that fills this small side canyon.

Mount Gorgeous required a huge amount of work to develop. Not only did the routes themselves require a large amount of cleaning, but the base and the approach trail took days of work. The first ascent credit shown does not come close to crediting all those who helped out. The following individuals make up "the gang" listed: Ben Banks, Joe Kristy, John Long, Bill Leventhal, Matt Oliphant, Lewis Weekland and several others.

Traci Marx on the final bulge of **Gorgeous** 10a/b****.

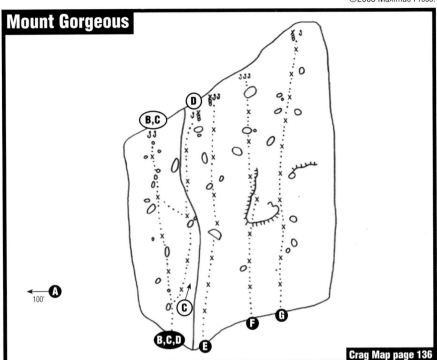

Mount Gorgeous

Crag Map page 136

Mount Gorgeous
Malibu Creek Intro: Page 128.

A. K-2 9**
4 bolts to 1 open shut and 1 biner. Climb the pocketed orange face, starting off a flat-topped boulder.
FA: John Long and the gang, 2001.

B. Luscious 11c/d**
4 bolts to 2 open shuts. Start on the left edge of the rounded corner, just left of the colorful lichen strip, and climb up to a high 1ˢᵗ bolt. From here continue up and left following steep jugs.
FA: Unknown.

C. Camel Straight 12a**
5 bolts to 2 open shuts. A link-up. Begin on *Cig-arete* and after clipping its 3ʳᵈ bolt move left to join *Luscious* for its last 2 bolts.
FA: Jeff Constine, 2001.

D. Cig-arete 11b*
5 bolts to 1 open shut and 1 chain. Start as for *Luscious*, but at the top of the slab climb right to the 1ˢᵗ bolt. Climb the overhanging arete and face above. Somewhat height dependent.
FA: Bill Leventhal and the gang, 2001.

E. Gorgeous 10a/b****
7 bolts to 2 open shuts and 1 biner or 1 open shut and 1 biner. Climb up the slabby buttress to a dished area at mid-height. After resting here, pull through the steep bulge above. A very popular route. ➤ Photo facing page.
FA: John Long and the gang, 2001.

F. Family Jewel 10c/d***
7 bolts to 3 open shuts. Begin 15 feet to the right of *Gorgeous* and climb the steep slab past 3 bolts to a huge hole. The route climbs left above this hole and continues up the steep headwall.
FA: John Long and the gang, 2001.

G. Delicious 10d/11a*****
10 bolts to 1 open shut and 1 chain. The best route on the wall. Start climbing a few feet to the right of *Family Jewel*, eventually reaching the same huge hole found on that route. From here climb up and right through a series of bulges to the top of the formation. ➤ Photo facing page.
FA: Matt Oliphant and the gang, 2001.

Tony Sartin entering the slab crux of **Lonesome Stranger** 11d/12a**.

The Ghetto
C. Skeezer Pleaser 11b★★★★
J. Maximum Ghetto 13a★★★
L. Johnny Can't Lead 11b★★★★
P. Urban Struggle 12a/b★★★★
T. Ghetto Blaster 13a★★★★★

Crag Map page 136

The Ghetto

Malibu Creek State Park Intro: Page 128. Prior to recent developments this was the only real lead wall in the Park. This is still one of the most popular areas and offers the highest concentration of steep and difficult routes. Some of the more recent routes added make this a much more attractive wall with lower level leaders than it once was. The wall is in the shade in the morning and early afternoon. **Topo:** See next page.

A. Street Science 12c★★★

3 bolts to 2 open shuts. Climbs up and through the big pod at the far left of the wall.
FA: Steve Edwards, 1994.

B. Lonesome Stranger 11d/12a★★

5 bolts to a double biner anchor. Starts up the vertical vein of pockets just right of *Street Science* before cutting left at a huge dish/cave. Climb into the body-sized pod and turn its roof on jugs. ➤ Photo facing page.
FA: Tony Sartin, 2001.

C. Skeezer Pleaser 11b★★★★

5 bolts to 2 open shuts. Steep jugs lead to a bouldery crux at the end. Very popular.
➤ Photo page 143, rear cover.
FA: Louie Anderson, 1991.

D. Directpissima 11a★★

6 bolts to a double biner anchor. The direct finish to *Kathmandu*, climbing up and left at either the 3rd or 4th bolt of that route.
FA: Aaron Lennox, Tony Sartin, 2002.

Continued next page.

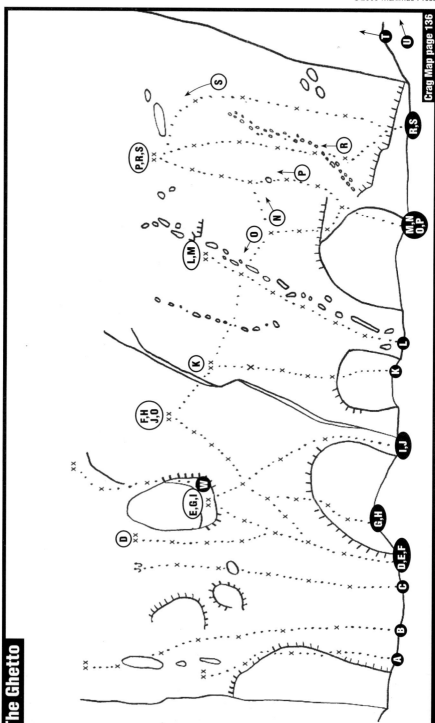

Crag Map page 136

The Ghetto

ne Ghetto

Descriptions for routes A through D are found on the previous page.

E. Kathmandu 10b**

4 bolts to 2 chains. The original route on the wall. Fun pocket climbing leads to chains at the base of the upper cave.

FA: Dave Katz, Mark Bowling, 1985.

F. Ghetto Crossing 13a***

8 bolts to 2 chains. Climbs *Kathmandu*, but after clipping its 2nd bolt traverse right over the cave and finish up *Maximum Ghetto*. ➤ Photo page 131.

FA: Aaron Lennox, 2002.

G. Brenna 13c/d**

5 bolts to 2 chains. Start climbing 8 feet right of *Kathmandu* (in the cave). Climb through the roof and finish on *Stun Gun*.

FA: Sean Diamond, 2001.

H. Lateralus 14a****

8 bolts to 2 chains. Start as for *Brenna*, but finish up *Maximum Ghetto*. Currently the hardest route in the Park.

FA: Sean Diamond, 2002.

I. Stun Gun 12c/d**

3 bolts to 2 chains. Climb up vertical pods until it is possible to move left onto the face. The route climbs left for about ten feet before heading straight up on small pockets to the chains.

FA: John Mireles, Bill Leventhal, 1991.

J. Maximum Ghetto 13a***

6 bolts to 2 chains. Start as for *Stun Gun*, but after clipping its 2nd bolt climb up and right over a small bulge. The original Malibu testpiece.

FA: John Mireles,1991.

K. Darkest Hour 12c**

4 bolts to 2 chains. Named in remembrance of John Yablonski's suicide, this route climbs up and right, diagonally. The original line stayed low, but most people climb a higher series of pockets.

FA: John Mireles, 1992.

L. Johnny Can't Lead 11b****

5 bolts to 2 open shuts. The other original route. Follows a perfect vein of juggy pockets to the now-higher anchors. Another very popular route.

FA: Dave Katz, Tom Grimes, 1985.

M. Hole Patrol 12b**

5 bolts to 2 chains. Begin at the start of *Urban Struggle*, but after clipping its 1st bolt climb up and left, through the roof and continue left to finish on Johnny Can't Lead.

FA: John Mireles, Bill Leventhal, 1991.

N. Stink Finger 12c***

7 bolts to 2 chains. Start as for *Hole Patrol*, but after clipping its 4th bolt head back right via a cross through to a mono. Finish up *Urban Struggle*.

FA: Wills Young, 1992.

O. Toxeth Walk 12c

7 bolts to 2 open shuts. Climb *Hole Patrol*, however instead of finishing at the anchors of *Johnny Can't Lead* continue to the anchors of *Maximum Ghetto*.

FA: Kevin Thaw, 1992.

P. Urban Struggle 12a/b****

6 bolts to 2 chains. After clipping the 1st bolt traverse right along the flat shelf. From the end of the shelf follow a beautiful line of pockets through an otherwise blank face. An optional start features a jump to the flat jug at the end of the shelf (after stick clipping the 2nd bolt). A real crowd pleaser.

FA: John Mireles, Bill Leventhal, 1991.

Q. Suburban Struggle 11b**(r)

5 bolts to 2 chains. An easier way to get through the middle of *Urban Struggle* is to climb right following larger pockets before rejoining it higher up. Seldom done due to the runout.

FA: Kevin Thaw, 1992.

R. Urban Sprawl 10a/b**

5 bolts to 2 chains. Traverse in from the right and then climb the mostly vertical face to the anchors of *Urban Struggle*.

FA: Aaron Lennox, Tony Sartin, 2002.

S. Junk Ramp 9

4 bolts to 2 open shuts. The name says it all!

FA: Bill Leventhal,1991.

T. Ghetto Blaster 13a*****

7 bolts to anchors on the ledge above. The best route on the wall! Start around the corner from *Junk Ramp* and climb up the overhanging, streaked wall to a funky topout.

➤ Photo page 19.

FA: Eddie Yanik, 1995.

U. Ground Zero 12a**

5 bolts to a double biner anchor. Start around to the right of *Ghetto Blaster* and follow a series of smooth cobbles and sidepulls, followed by the crux deadpoint. A nice new route, with a different flavor from the other routes.

➤ Photo page 2.

FA: Tony Sartin 2001.

V. Tony's Project

Bolts up a long, steep wall.

EB: Tony Sartin.

W. Dead Rats 9

2 bolts to 2 bolt anchor. Climb the short ramp above the *Kathmandu* anchors.

FA: Bill Leventhal, 1991.

The Wave
B. Hosed 11d*
D. Pocket Jones 11c****
E. Pocket Pool 11c***

Matt Oliphant on **Amphetamine** 11b***.

The Wave

Malibu Creek State Park Intro: Page 128. This 60 foot high, slightly overhung wall is approached via a 5-10 minute hike up the canyon just opposite The Ghetto. From The Ghetto, hike 100 feet downstream, and then move across and through the gigantic boulders in the streambed. Immediately after *Kim Chi* start up a trail in the steep gully/chute. After the initial few minutes the trail becomes more solid and less steep. Continue winding through the trees heading up and left (passing the ruins of an old treehouse). In a few minutes the wall (hidden from below) comes into view. Due to the afternoon shade found on its routes, the Wave is the obvious finish to a morning of climbing at one of the other walls.

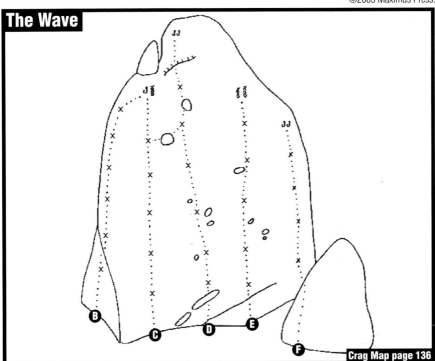

The Wave

A. Kim Chi 11d
6 bolts to a double chain anchor. Found in the creekbed immediately before heading uphill to The Wave. An old top-rope that has been turned into a short sport route (short, despite the fact that it has as many bolts as the much longer routes at The Ghetto across the canyon).
EB: Ki Bum. FA: John Long, 2002.

B. Hosed 11d*
6 bolts to 1 open shut and 1 biner belay. Looks easier than it is. Start just left of the left-hand arete and climb up and right following the arete itself and the face immediately right of it. Finishes with a funky traverse right to the anchors of *Amphetamine*.
FA: John Long, Joe Kristy, 2002.

C. Amphetamine 11b***
6 or 7 bolts to anchors. Follows line of thin pockets right of *Hosed*. From the 5th bolt either head straight up to the shuts, or traverse right and follow *Pocket Jones* past 2 more bolts to its anchor. ➤ Photo facing page.
FA: Dan Hauglestine, 1996.

D. Pocket Jones 11c****
8 bolts to 2 open shuts. A few thin moves between big pockets to an exciting bulge finish. The best route on the wall and very popular.
FA: Dan Hauglestine, 1996.

E. Pocket Pool 11c***
5 bolts to a double biner anchor. Slightly smaller holds than those found on *Pocket Jones*, but with moves that aren't as reachy. Another great route up the steep wall. It's best to climb a move past the anchors to clip.
➤ Photo this page.
FA: John Long, Joe Kristy, 2002.

F. Blast 11a/b**
4 bolts to 2 open shuts. The right-hand arete. Climb up the slabby formation on the right until the first bolt can be clipped. Continue up the arete on large flat holds and jugs.
FA: Dan Hauglestine, 1996.

Bill Leventhal on **Pocket Pool** 11c***.

©2003 Maximus Press.

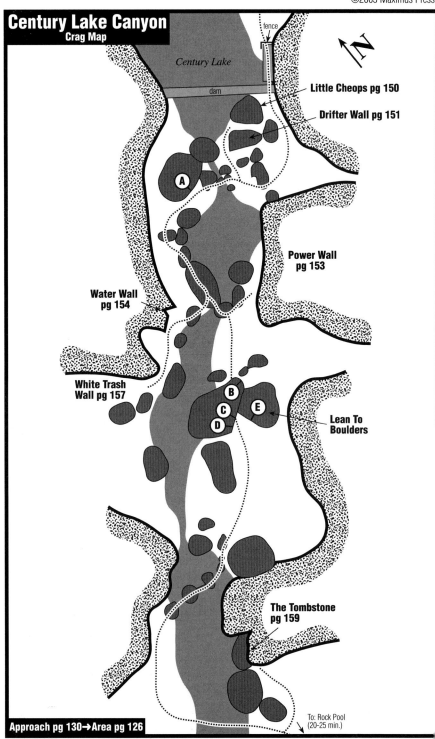

Century Lake Canyon
Crag Map

Century Lake

fence

N

dam

Little Cheops pg 150

Drifter Wall pg 151

A

Power Wall
pg 153

Water Wall
pg 154

White Trash
Wall pg 157

B

C

E

D

Lean To
Boulders

The Tombstone
pg 159

Approach pg 130→Area pg 126

To: Rock Pool
(20-25 min.)

Century Lake Canyon

Malibu Creek State Park Intro: Page 128. The most recently developed collection of routes in the Park can be found just beyond the Century Lake Dam. More a collection of developed faces than an individual crag, Century Lake Canyon provides the most diverse collection of sport routes found in Malibu Creek. Most of the routes found here are in the shade in the morning and early afternoon, with the exception of the Water Wall, which is in the sun most of the day. Due to the relatively new nature of the routes found here, the quality ratings shown will only stand true with the moderate cleaning that occurs with a route's initial traffic and weathering.

A. L.A. Blues 11b/c**(tr)

Climb out the cave and continue on the steep, upper face.

John Long on **Swamp Thing** 12c***.

ean To Boulders

The appropriately named Lean To Boulders are located downstream from the Water Wall, on the same side of the water as the Power Wall. They are made up of two large boulders that are leaning against each other. The routes are located in the corridor between the two boulders.

. Swamp Thing 12c***

bolts to 1 open shut and 1 biner. Starts down in the pit and climbs past bouldery pocket sequences up and right more positive holds on the arete. ➤ Photo this page.
John Long, Matt Oliphant, Mike Draper, 1999.

. Pick Pocket 11b**

bolts to 2 open shuts. Climbs the center of the steep ce, following a line of huge pockets.
Matt Oliphant, Mike Draper, 1999.

. Wild Willie 11b*(tr)

mbs the left arete.
Matt Dansby, Mark Wilford, 1987.

. Eiger Sanction 11b/c(tr)

mb the overhanging rounded arete through 2 scooped ctions. Dirty and not recommended.
Mark Wilford, 1987.

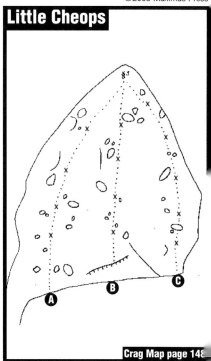

Crag Map page 148

Matt Callender onsighting **The Drifter** 12a****

Little Cheops

Malibu Creek State Park Intro: Page 128. The following routes are found in the narrow corridor located between the two large boulders closest to the dam. Climb up out of the creekbed about ten feet to enter the corridor. Little Cheops is in the shade until late morning.

A. Mummy 10b*
5 bolts to 1 biner and 1 open shut. This route starts at the top of the approach chimney and climbs the vertical face above to a high crux.
FA: John Long, Joe Kristy, 2002.

B. Tut 10b**
5 bolts to 1 biner and 1 open shut. Start climbing off a small ledge and continue straight up the middle of the wall.
FA: John Long, Joe Kristy, 2002.

C. Scarab 9***
5 bolts to 1 biner and 1 open shut. Climbs the right arete and the face just to its left.
FA: John Long, Joe Kristy, 2002.

Drifter Wall
B. The Drifter 12a*****

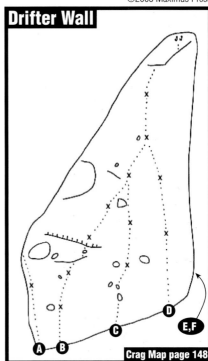

Drifter Wall

Crag Map page 148

Drifter Wall

Malibu Creek State Park Intro: Page 128. The steep routes found on this large rock are highly visible when hiking down from the dam. Caution should be taken when climbing these routes due to the boulders located directly behind the climber. A very pleasant midday hang can be found in the caves and tunnels to the right of *Fallout's* base. All routes enjoy morning shade.

A. Unnamed 10?
1 bolt, lower off a thread through two adjacent huecos. Climb up the arete passing a single bolt until established on the less than vertical face above.
Bill Leventhal, 1993.

B. The Drifter 12a*****
7 bolts to shared 2 open shuts. Start near the left edge of the face and climb up and right to a steep bulge. Climb through this crux bulge and continue up and right to the top of the wall. Excellent!
Photo page 124, facing page.
Louie Anderson, 2002.

C. Aftermath 11d***
bolts to shared 2 open shuts. A direct start to *The Drifter* that avoids its crux.
Louie Anderson, 2002.

D. Fallout 11c***
4 bolts to shared 2 open shuts. The far right route. Climb past bouldery moves to a series of edges that eventually join *The Drifter* at its 6th bolt.
FA: Louie Anderson, 2002.

E. The Shadow 11b**
4 bolts to 2 shared open shuts. Begin climbing just around the corner from *Fallout*. Climb up and right following big pockets. Somewhat dark.
FA: Louie Anderson, 2002.

F. Dark Star 10d*
4 bolts to 2 shared open shuts. Climb directly below the anchors of *The Shadow*, clipping the last bolt of that route. Somewhat dark.
FA: Chris Murray, 2002.

Power Wall
A. Power Grid 10b**
C. Rolling Blackout 10d****
G. Electric Eye 10b/c**

Bryan Lorentzen on **Rolling Blackout** 10d***

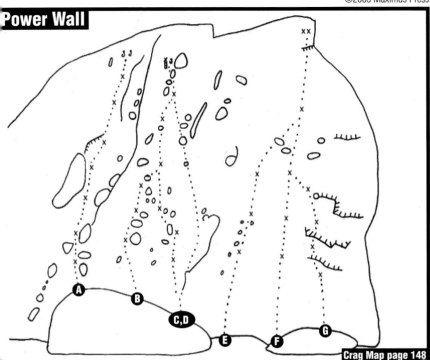

Power Wall

Crag Map page 148

ower Wall

lalibu Creek State Park Intro: Page 28. A towering wall that would have vice as many routes if it weren't for the rge pond at its left base. The routes ere can conveniently be done from a rge flat-topped boulder while keeping ur rope out of the surrounding water. ne only exception to this is *Power Grid*, hich requires a quick hand when ulling the rope. The wall is in the shade til early afternoon.

. **Power Grid** 10b★★

olts to 2 open shuts. Traverse left over the water before mbing up between two large fins. Climb around the left and continue up the vertical face above.
Jeff Constine, Bill Leventhal, 2002.

. **Power Station** 10b★★★

olts to shared open shut and biner anchor. Climbs the ep, right-leaning face 10 feet left of *Rolling Blackout*, sing several huge huecos. Shares the last three bolts Rolling Blackout.
Bill Leventhal, Matt Oliphant, 2001.

C. **Rolling Blackout** 10d★★★★

6 bolts to shared open shut and biner anchor. The best route on the wall! Climb through several steep bulges on jugs. ➤ Photo facing page.
FA: Bill Leventhal, Matt Oliphant, 2001.

D. **Power Outage** 11d★★(tr)

Climb up and stand on top of the fin. Climb the inside face of a big pod and over a small bulge before going left to finish up *Rolling Blackout*.
FTR: Bill Leventhal, 2001.

E. **Powder Puff Girls** 9★★

4 bolts to a shared double bolt anchor. Climb diagonally right up the smooth slab and continue up a steeper finish to anchors on a ledge.
FA: Jeff and Fumie Constine, 2002.

F. **Power Ranger** 9★

4 bolts to a shared double bolt anchor. Starts 5 feet left of *Electric Eye* and climbs straight up using several large pockets. Finish as for *Powder Puff Girls*.
FA: Jeff and Fumie Constine, 2002.

6. **Electric Eye** 10b/c★★

6 bolts to a shared double bolt anchor. Climbs the smooth face at the far right of the wall, using blocky holds and underclings. Finish as for *Powder Puff Girls*.
FA: Jeff Constine, Bill Leventhal, 2002.

Water Wall
B. Fissure Man 10c***
D. Waterworld 10b**

Crag Map page 148

Water Wall

Malibu Creek State Park Intro: Page 128. Located across and slightly down stream from the Power Wall, the Water Wall can easily be identified by the crack found on the upper half of Fissure Man. While only partially develope (the face around and to the left will no doubt have future routes), the existin routes are quite enjoyable and different in nature from other Malibu Cree routes. Once again, be careful when pulling your rope to keep it out of th water. The Water Wall is in the sun from mid-morning on.

A. Water's Edge 11c**(tr)

Bolt anchor on ledge above requires approximately 20-foot extender rope. Start as for *Fissure Man*, but instead of following the crack to the right, climb up the left arete.
FA: Bill Leventhal, 2001.

B. Fissure Man 10c***

6 bolts to shared 2 open shuts. Climb up the heavily pocketed slab before following the crack on the upper face. A very unique route for the Park.
FA: Bill Leventhal, 2001.

C. Water Boy 10c/d***(r)

8 bolts to shared 2 open shuts. A direct start to *Fissure Man* that climbs a steep face on juggy pockets. The ram behind and to the left is off route and care should be tak not to hit it in case of a fall. Climb past the 4th bolt until established on the face above it and then traverse left to finish up the crack of *Fissure Man*.
FA: Louie Anderson, 2002.

D. Waterworld 10b**(r)

4 bolts to 2 open shuts. Start as for *Water Boy*, but after clipping its 4th bolt climb straight up instead of traversir left. ➤ Photo facing page.
FA: Louie Anderson, 2002.

Stein Lundby on **Waterworld** 10b**.

White Trash Wall
B. White Trash 13a****
E. Bubba 9**

Bryan Lorentzen enters the crux of **White Trash** 13a***

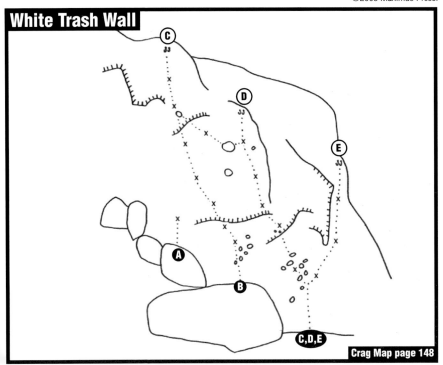

White Trash Wall

Crag Map page 148

White Trash Wall

Malibu Creek Intro: Page 128. The wall sees shade until mid day.

A. Project

1 bolt so far.

B. White Trash 13a★★★★

7 bolts to 2 shared open shuts. This route should be considered a serious lead due to the close proximity of the large boulders below the route. Belayers are strongly urged to make use of the belay bolt at the base of the cave's rear wall. Climb up to the roof using huge jugs. After clipping the 2nd bolt, power through the crux deadpoint and continue on sustained edge climbing to the anchors. ➤ Photo facing page, page 160.
FA: Louie Anderson, 2002.

C. Trailer Trash 12b★★★

3 bolts to 2 shared open shuts. A link-up. Begin on *Trailer Park* and traverse straight left after its 5th bolt, passing 1 independent bolt. Joins *White Trash* at its 6th bolt.
FA: Louie Anderson, 2002.

D. Trailer Park 11c★★★

5 bolts to 2 open shuts. Start off the ground and climb through a heavily-huecoed section. Traverse left through a bulge and continue up the steep arete above.
➤ Photo this page.
FA: Louie Anderson, 2002.

E. Bubba 9★★

3 bolts to 2 open shuts. This route begins as for *Trailer Park*, but clips a different first bolt before climbing up and right into the steep dihedral.
FA: Louie Anderson, 2002.

Mark Fekkes on **Trailer Park** 11c★★★.

Chris Murray on **Epitaph** 11b**.

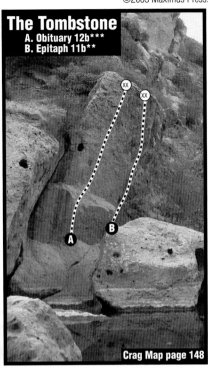

The Tombstone
A. Obituary 12b***
B. Epitaph 11b**

Crag Map page 148

The Tombstone

Malibu Creek State Park Intro: Page 128. This prominent overhung block is home to two very enjoyable routes. Care should be taken when pulling your rope on both routes as they begin directly above the water.

A. Obituary 12b***

4 bolts to 2 open shuts. This route begins off the large flat shelf just above the water and climbs the smooth, pocketed face above passing a sloping ledge towards the bottom. Expect some powerful pocket pulls on this one.
➤ Photo this page.
FA: Louie Anderson, 2002.

B. Epitaph 11b**

5 bolts to 2 open shuts. Start at a group of large pockets and climb straight up to the arete above. Follow the layback fin until it ends and then continue on flat edges to the anchors. ➤ Photo facing page.
FA: Louie Anderson, 2002.

Doniel Drazin on **Obituary** 12b***.

See Page 157

Louie Anderson on **White Trash** 13a****. *Matt Callender Photo.*

Andy Meadors on **Planet of the Apes** 11a****. *John Bereza Photo.*

See Page 135

Mash Boulder

Malibu Creek State Park Intro: Page 128. This 25-foot tall boulder is found by hiking about 20-30 minutes past Century Lake on the fire road. It is easy to pass and the point where the approach trail leaves the main trail is easily missed. The top of the boulder can be seen over the trees on the opposite side of the creekbed. If you reach the Mash Site (marked by the remains of an old Army Jeep and utility truck) you know you've gone too far. There are bolts on top of the boulder for setting up a toprope. The routes are on extremely clean, overhung rock and are quite good.

A. Section Eight 12d***(tr)
Climb *Malibu Swinger*, but with the direct finish instead of traversing around it.
FA: John Mireles, 1991.

B. Malibu Swinger 12c**(tr)
The difficult left hand route. Traverse left at the top in order to avoid the final difficulties.
FA: Bill Leventhal, Neil Kaptain, 1989.

C. Kicking the Nam Syndrome 13a***(tr)
The original route envisioned on the wall. Climb the steep center of the face.
FA: Wills Young, 1994.

D. Cross Dresser 12c/d**(tr)
Begin climbing on *Corporal Klinger*, but shortly after beginning traverse left to finish up *Section Eight*.
FA: John Mireles, 1991.

E. Corporal Klinger 11d***(tr)
Climbs the right side of the face. The original classic on the boulder.
FA: Bill Leventhal, Neil Kaptain, 1989.

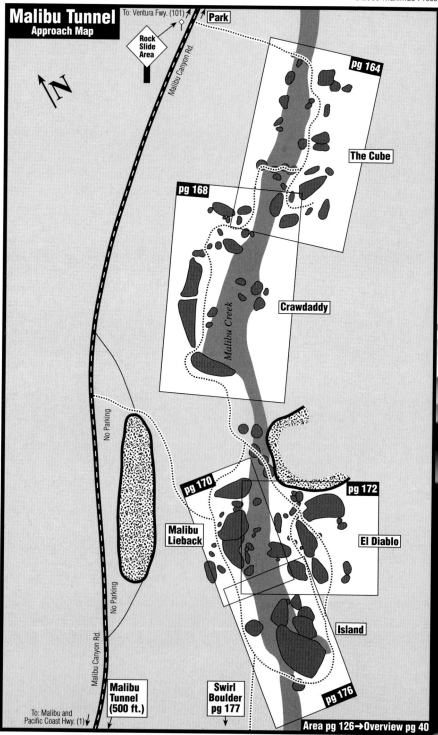

Malibu Tunnel
Approach Map

N

To: Ventura Fwy. (101)

Park

Rock
Slide
Area

Malibu Canyon Rd.

pg 164

The Cube

pg 168

Crawdaddy

Malibu Creek

No Parking

No Parking

Malibu Canyon Rd.

pg 170

pg 172

Malibu
Lieback

El Diablo

Island

pg 176

Malibu
Tunnel
(500 ft.)

To: Malibu and
Pacific Coast Hwy. (1)

Swirl
Boulder
pg 177

Area pg 126→Overview pg 40

Malibu Tunnel

There are a few highball problems found here. Most of the taller boulders have bolts or other fixed gear, or adjacent trees that can be tied off to allow for top-roping. The landings are pretty nice, although a few consist of jumbled boulders and a pad can make them better. The area is very convenient and one can be bouldering 15 minutes after leaving the car.

Malibu Tunnel Details

Elevation: 400 ft.
Exposure: Varied, sun and shade.
Bouldering: 108 problems, VB to V8.
Drive From the 101: 15 minutes.
Drive From Hwy 1: 10 minutes
Approach: 15 to 25 minute walk.

History: The boulders found in the creekbed just north of the Malibu Tunnel were quite popular from the mid 80s until the early 90s. In the last few years several new and harder problems have been added and the area is now enjoying a bit of renewed interest.

The Approach: Park in the paved parking area just south of Piuma Road and the Tapia Water Reclamation Facility. Cross the road (carefully) and walk south on Malibu Canyon Road for about 10 minutes. There is a large orange and blue "peace" sign graffiti painted on a diamond shaped boulder high on the hillside directly above The Cube. Just before reaching this look for a sign that says "Rock Slide Area" on the opposite side of the road. Directly across from this sign (and adjacent to a power pole with yellow cable supports) a steep trail leads down to the beginning of the developed bouldering.

See Page 165

Louie Anderson on his problem **Full Throttle** V8*****. *Jeff Truman Photo.*

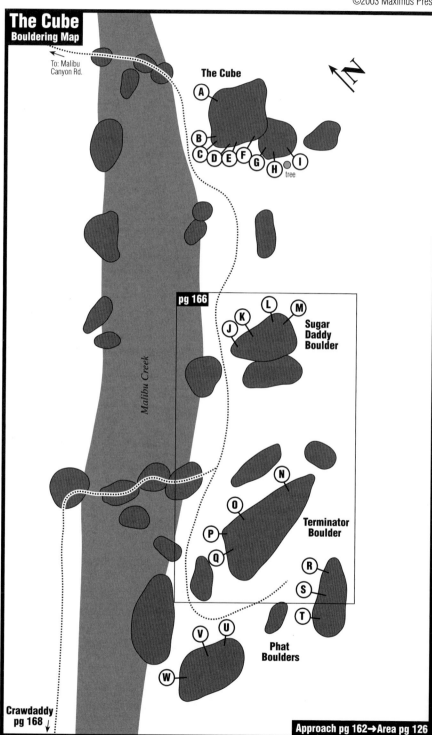

The Cube
Bouldering Map

To: Malibu
Canyon Rd.

The Cube

A

B
C D E F G H I
tree

pg 166

J K L M
Sugar
Daddy
Boulder

N

O

P

Q

Terminator
Boulder

R

S

T

V U

W

Phat
Boulders

Crawdaddy
pg 168

Approach pg 162→Area pg 126

The Cube

The Cube
Malibu Tunnel Intro: Page 163.

A. Full Powder V6***
Start at the far left and traverse the lip around both sides of the boulder, before topping out.

B. Blockhead V3**
Jump to the corner and mantle.

C. Powder Edge V2**
Jump to the corner and traverse the lip right to the end of the boulder.

D. Backfire V4**
Start in pockets on arete and climb face.

E. Thrust V6****
Climb steep pocketed arete to sloping topout.

F. Full Throttle V8*****
Begin at circular portion of rail deep in cave and traverse left to arete and topout of *Thrust*. ➤ Photo page 163.

G. Hot Rod V0*
Start with right hand in pocket and climb face.

H. Street Legal V1**
Start off the top of a small boulder with the left hand on the arete and the right on a blocky sloper. High step the right foot.

I. Le Coif V5****
Dead hang, matched on the big flat edge behind the tree. Campus to lip sloper and traverse to finish on *Street Legal*. A harder variation (V7) starts matched low on the right edge of the boulder and traverses into the regular problem. ➤ Photo page 167.

Phat Boulders
R. Phat Albert V0*
Sit start. Follow diagonal seam to jugs.

S. Phat Cat V2**
Sit start matched on slopey ramp. Variation: go to lip before reaching jugs.

T. Phat Cow V3*
Start as for *Phat Cat*, but go with the right hand to a sloping crimp from the starting holds.

U. Knob Job V1*
Sit start with right hand in sloping dish and left hand on big cobble. Follow line of knobs.

V. Gadzooks V0*
Sit start with left hand on cobble and right hand in big gaston. Climb the featured face.

W. Holey Moley V1*
Sit start matched in big hole and climb the pocketed face.

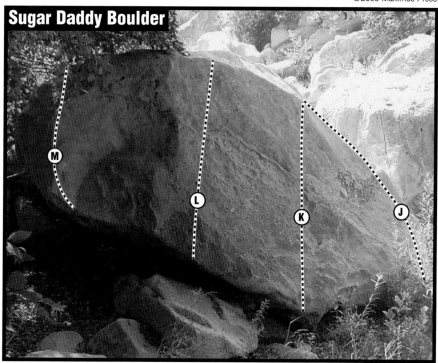

Sugar Daddy Boulder

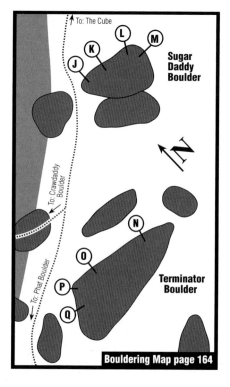

Bouldering Map page 164

Sugar Daddy Boulder
Malibu Tunnel Intro: Page 163.

J. Sole Sister VB**
Climb smooth right arete.
K. Sole Food V0-**
Climb smooth slab. Arete off.
L. Sole Power VB*
Featured slab.
M. Sugar Daddy V0+*
Sit start matched on edge in overhang. The right variation is V2*.

Terminater Boulder
N. Terminator V7****
Sit start matched on low pocket. Climb up and right on knobs and pockets.
O. Procrastinator V3***
Sit start matched on flake. Climbs knobs and sidepulls. Arete off.
P. Enforcer V1-**
Sit start and climb pocketed arete and then right on pockets.
Q. Violator VB*
Sit start matched in large pocket.

See Page 165

Jeff Truman on the First Ascent of the regular version of **Le Coif** V5****.

Terminator Boulder

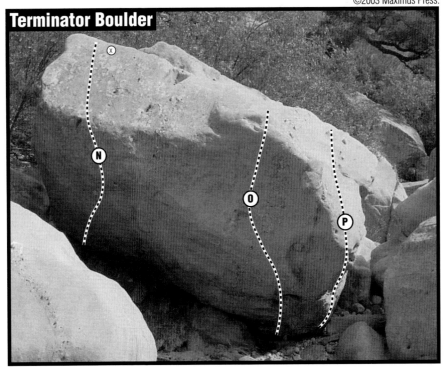

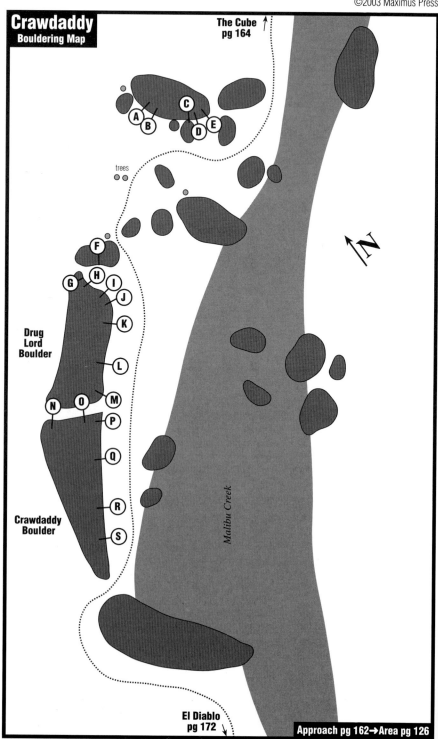

Crawdaddy
Bouldering Map

The Cube
pg 164

A B C D E

trees

F
G H I J K
Drug
Lord
Boulder
L
N O M
P
Q
Crawdaddy
Boulder
R
S

Malibu Creek

N

El Diablo
pg 172

Approach pg 162→Area pg 126

Crawdaddy Boulder

A. Pipe Dream V2*
Starts right next to drain pipe. Sit start with hands on sloping crimps over the lip.
B. Cobble in a Dish V1+**
Sit start matched in the namesake hold. Climb up to arete.
C. Space Shuttle V3***
Match on a rail. Throw left to diagonal edge and topout.
D. Lost in Space V1**
Start matched on higher flat edge and move to right hand sidepull.
E. Man in the Moon V2**
Sit start with left hand in hole and right hand on lip crimp. Climb over bulge.

Drug Lord Boulder
F. Overdose V3***
Start on the flat edge at the far left and traverse the lip before topping out.
G. Slum Lord V3*
Climb right facing corner. Start right hand in pocket or edge.
H. Kingpin V2**(highball)
Climb stemming corner, starting on left edge.
I. Drug Lord V3****
Start on head high flat edge. Climb face with orange knob.

J. Buzz Saw V0+**
Climb right side of arete.
K. Freebase V0*
Climb arete using knob for right hand.
L. Redstone V1+*(h)
Face to shallow left facing corner.
M. The Junkie V0*
Climb left arete.

Crawdaddy Boulder
N. Barracuda V2***(h)
Start matched on horizontal. Climb steep face and right arete.
O. King Crab V5***(h)
Right side of sharp right arete. Back boulder off.
P. Flyweenakiss V2***(h)
Left side of sharp right arete.
Q. Crawdaddy V3-*
Climb face 5 feet left of arete.
R. Flydaddy V0+**
Face with small ramp at mid height.
S. Rock Lobster V2**
Sit start matched on the sloping rail. Cross knobs up and left to another small ramp.

Jeff Truman on **Fear Factor** V3***.

Stacy Goncharko on **Small Fry** V1*.

See Page 172

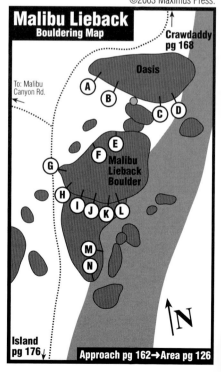

Malibu Lieback
Bouldering Map

Crawdaddy
pg 168

Oasis

To: Malibu
Canyon Rd.

A

B

C   D

E

F   Malibu
Lieback
Boulder

G

H

I   J   K   L

M

N

N

Island
pg 176

Approach pg 162→Area pg 126

Malibu Lieback Boulder

Oasis
Malibu Tunnel Intro: Page 163.

A. Oasis V2+**
Edge of shallow dihedral.

B. Bouldering for Dollars V1+**
Climb edges up face.

C. Smoke and Mirrors V4**
Start right hand in 2 finger pocket and left on sloping edge. Climb arete above.

D. Mirage V8***
Jump start to sloping ledge.

Malibu Lieback Boulder
E. Starvation V6**
Climb steep face on thin holds.

F. Overlord V4***
Undercling big hueco and climb arete.

G. The Prow V8***?
Ground has lowered considerably over the years. A difficult lower start is possible. Unclimbed as is?

H. Avalon V6**
Start at the left end of the shelf and climb over the bulge.

I. Crocodile Rock V2*
Climb right edge of steep face.

J. Malibu Lieback VB**(highball)
Climb the obvious lieback crack.

K. Giant Steps Unfold V2**(h)
Start in the leftmost pockets. Climb over the roof and up the slab.

L. Department of Water and Power (DWP) V1+*
Start in pockets and climb up and right.

M. Fear Factor V3***
Start matched on the big, rounded knob under the roof. Throw to sloping lip and topout. ➤ Photo facing page.

N. Fraidy Cat V2+**
Start matched on lower lip sloper. Move to horizontal and top out.

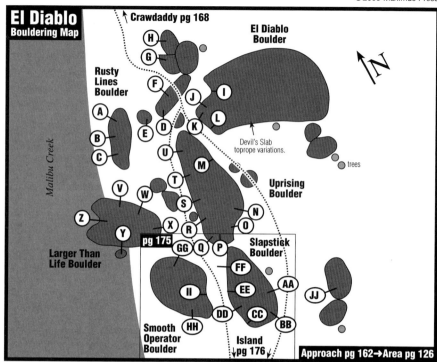

Rusty Lines Boulder
Malibu Tunnel Intro: Page 163.

A. Friction V2**
Start left hand on the big, triangle-shaped sloper at chest height.

B. Rusty Lines V7***
Climb the center of the smooth face. Jump variation (from the ground) to high right hold is V2 **

C. Jumping Jack V0*
Start on horizontal rust streak and jump to high right hold (arete off).

D. Shell Arete V1*
Climb the arete with fossilized shells and small pockets.

E. Junkyard Dog V2+**
Sit start off the boulder, matched on flat edge. Climb the sloping edges.

F. Simple Simon V0+*
Sit start and climb past sloping pockets.

G. Small Fry V1*
Sit start. Climb steep arete. ➤ Photo page 170.

H. Flat Funk V0**
Sit start matched on the flat ledge. The left rock underneath is OK to use; the right round one is off.

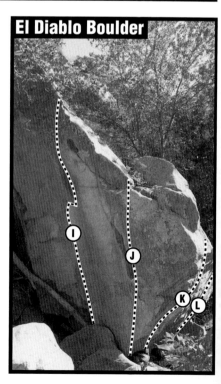

El Diablo Boulder

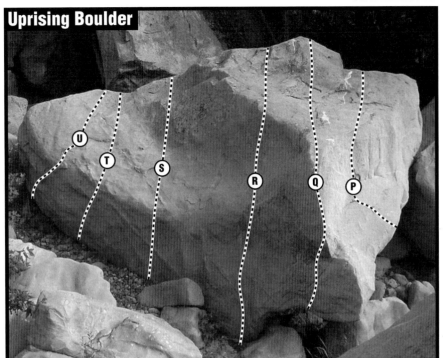

Uprising Boulder

El Diablo Boulder
I. El Diablo V3*****(highball)
The very clean dihedral. Its been bouldered, but most opt for a top-rope.
J. Hot Mama V2***
Start with your left hand in the 2 finger pocket and your right on the arete.
K. Lycra Boy V3****
Follow the big rail up and right. ➤ Photo page 174.
L. Lycra Man V7***
Sit start in undercling pockets and climb steep face to circular edge over the lip.

Uprising Boulder
M. Flake and Bake V2+**
Sit start matched on the left facing flake.
N. Tension V2**
Standing start with right hand on the crimp and the left on the arete.
O. Flyboy V3**
Start with the left hand on a low crimp and right on a pocket undercling. Do a move and then throw to the lip.
P. Uprising V7**
Sit start at left side of cave in underclings. Traverse up and left around bulge.

Q. Underdog V2*
Climb the right arete.
R. Mutiny V3**
Start right hand on the slopey pinch.
S. Power to the People V2**
Start matched on a small sloping rib over the lip.
T. Revolt V2**
Match start on lip and climb the face right of the flake.
U. Rebel Yell V2*
Start on head high crimps, then climb to and up the flake.

Larger Than Life Boulder
V. Bigger Than Big V0**
Climb right side of slab with diagonal slashes.
W. Massive V1**
Climb left side of slab with diagonal slashes.
X. Larger Than Life V7***
Start on chickenheads under roof. Move to undercling and then traverse left on underclings to sidepulls. Finish up slopey arete.
Y. The Great Divide V3***
Start climbing off small boulder in creek. Climb half-formed pockets up and right to the sloping rib.
Z. Test Tube V0**
Stem up the Polished Face.

See Page 173

Chris Murray on the steep rails of **Lycra Boy** V3****.

Slapstick Boulder
Malibu Tunnel Intro: Page 163.

AA. Slapstick V1+**
Climb out the scoop.

BB. Slaphappy V1***
Start crouched and slap up the right arete.

CC. Balancing Act V3***
Start on the right facing flake and mantle onto the upper slab.

DD. Like Glass V2**
Start with feet on edge by watermark and climb the slick face.

EE. Adam's Rib VO-*(highball)
Long slab with big, rust-colored rib.

FF. Eve VB*
Climb the left edge of the slab with a smaller rust-colored rib.

Smooth Operator Boulder

GG. Peakbagger VB*
Climb the featured slab.

HH. Smooth Operator V3***
Sit start and aim for the head high slopers.

II. Monkey Mantle V1**
Dead hang lip jug and mantle.

JJ. Groove Armada VO-*
Start low and climb face with big fins. Right boulder is off.

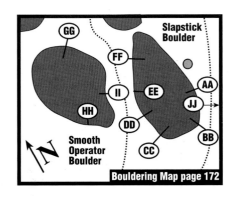

Bouldering Map page 172

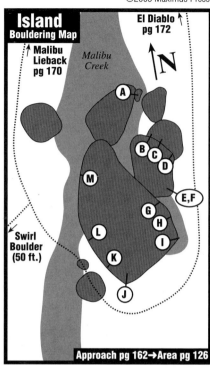

Island
Bouldering Map

El Diablo ↑
pg 172

↗ **Malibu**
Lieback
pg 170

Malibu
Creek

↑N

A

B C
D

M

E,F

G
H

L
I

Swirl
Boulder
(50 ft.)

K

J

Approach pg 162→Area pg 126

Island Boulder

A. Intimidation V3**
Start on head high sloper. Throw to hole and climb the slopey arete.

B. Teflon V4**
Sit start matched on right edge of scoop. Throw to sloper and topout up and left.
Variation: V7**. Right finish (left jugs are off).

C. Butterball V2**
Sit start using flat edge. Climb underclings up and left to sloping topout.

D. Under the Gun V2*
Sit start and climb the steep, huecoes on underclings.

E. The Scoop V0+**
Sit start and climb out the overhang on sidepulls and underclings.

F. Scoop Traverse V1***
Climb *The Scoop*, but traverse the lip to the right corner before topping out.

G. Apparatus V1+**(highball)
Climb the featured face. OK to stem off adjacent boulder.

H. Trash Compactor V4***(h)
Start with the left hand in the high undercling and the right on a small sloping edge. Paste your foot and cross. Beware the high mantle.

Island Boulder
East Face

I

H

G

F

E

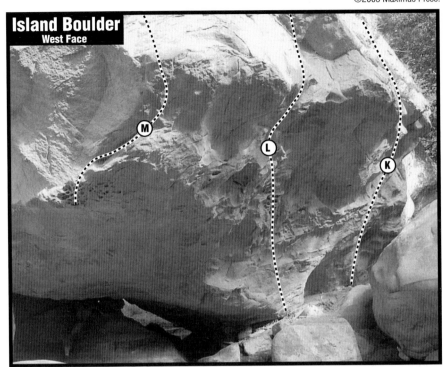

Island Boulder
West Face

I. Locals Only V2**(h)
Jump to right hold and climb to big hole, then up and left.
Left of *Locals Only* is a tall face offering good toprope options.

J. Crater Arete V0+**(h)
Sit start and follow the juggy arete finishing on the slab.

K. Luckyman V0+**(h)
Climb the steep chute over the boulder.

L. Islands in the Stream
V2+****(h)
Start on jugs and climb up and left through cave.

M. Launch V8***(h)
Jump to high pockets. Climb up and right. There is potential for a much lower cave start (climbing over the water).

Swirl Boulder

N. Swirl V3**
Start with left hand on the undercling and right on lip crimp. Traverse left along lip and climb left edge of face.

O. Tie-Dye V2*
Left hand starts on undercling and right on rib crimp. Climb the right arete.

P. Finger Function V0*
Sit start and climb the finger crack.

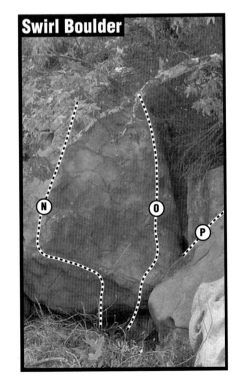

Swirl Boulder

See Page 185

Steve Edwards on the classic **Perro De La Guerra** 12c**** at Tick Rock.

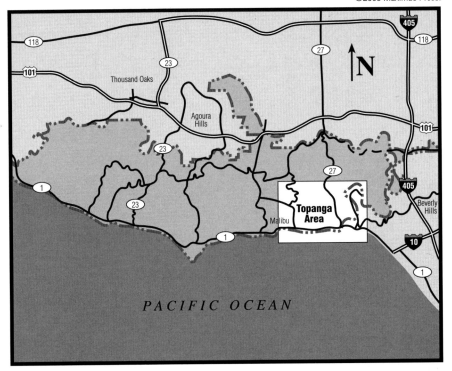

CHAPTER 4

TOPANGA AREA

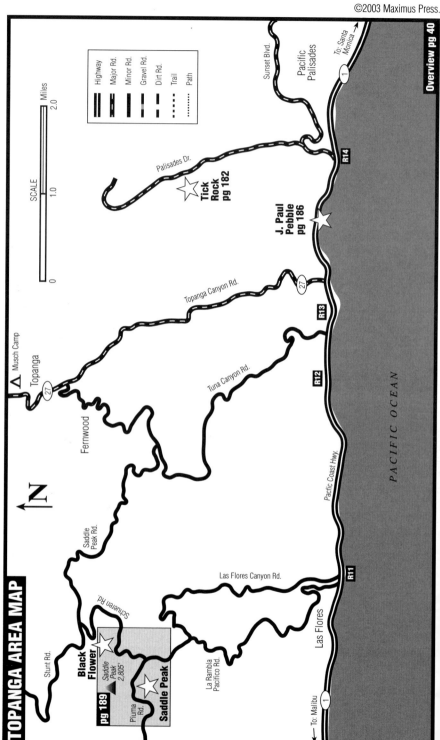

TOPANGA AREA BASICS

The Topanga Area's two main offerings, Tick Rock and Black Flower, are both extremely convenient and feature very short approaches. Because of this the area is an ideal selection for climbers that have only a partial day to climb, and are looking to maximize their time on the rock. Both areas also offer climbing styles that are vastly different from other Santa Monica Mountain areas.

Getting There

The crags in the Topanga Area are usually approached from the Pacific Coast Highway (1), but they can also be reached from the Ventura Freeway (101).

Restaurants

R11. Duke's
Seafood and steak.
21150 Pacific Coast Hwy.
☎ 310-317-0777

R12. Cholada Thai Cuisine
Authentic thai food with a beach flavor.
18763 Pacific Coast Hwy.
☎ 310-317-0025.

R13. Reel Inn Restaurant
Freshly caught seafood.
18661 Pacific Coast Hwy.
☎ 310-456-8221.

R14. Gladstones
Seafood and steak.
17300 Pacific Coast Hwy.
☎ 310-454-3474.

Camping

Musch Camp Hike-in
Open all year, the fee is $1. Picnic tables, piped water, flush toilets, no pets, elev. 1,300 ft. ☎ 800-444-7275.

Kenny Suh on **Zodiac** 11c*** at Black Flower.

See Page 191

See Page 185

Tom Wight on **Turning Point** 11d****.

Tick Rock

The Santa Monicas' "urban crag." This roadside formation sits smack dab in the middle of the ritzy Pacific Palisades community. There is a fair amount of rock in and around this area, but Tick Rock stands apart from the rest as being the most solid and the cleanest. The crag offers very fine

Tick Rock Details

Elevation: 600 ft.
Exposure: Varied, sun and shade.
Sport Climbs: 15 routes, 5.6 to 12c.
Drive From Hwy 1: 5 minutes
Approach: 5 minute hike.

grained sandstone, with routes up a heavily fractured and featured face. Most of the routes are much more reminiscent of granite climbing than the usual Southern California sandstone offerings. There is limited further potential here on the steep tower uphill to the left from the main formation.

There is also some limited bouldering available on the steep, blocky boulders below the crag. Most of the boulders and other faces on the surrounding hillsides are quite loose and dangerous.

Tick Rock's routes are in the shade in the early morning and in the afternoon, making the crag ideal for half-day excursions.

History: Since there has been climbing activity for some time, much of the first ascent information is unknown. However Darshan Etz and Abe are responsible for modernizing the crag and adding some variations in the late 90s

The Approach: Map page 180. The area is approached off the Pacific Coast Hwy. (1) by heading north on Sunset Blvd. The first traffic signal that you reach is Palisades Dr. Turn left here passing a small strip center on your right before entering a canyon. Roughly one and a half miles after turning onto Palisades Dr. the crag will be found on the left side of the road (just opposite a sign that reads "Rock Slide Area"). Only the top of the formation can be seen, as the majority of it lies in a depressed area behind the roadside hill. Either park in the large turnout area across the road or turn around and park under the trees directly below the crag. A steep trail leads up and over the small hill. The crag is reached in a matter of minutes from the car.

See Page 185

Carly Furuno on **Flying Guillotine** 10c***.

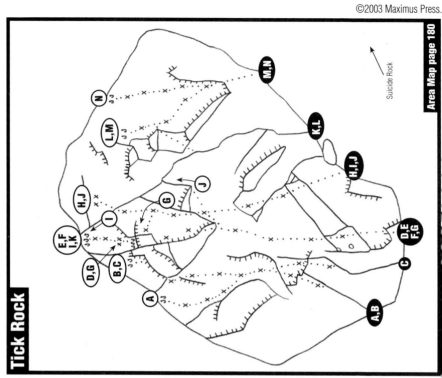

Tick Rock

Area Map page 180

Suicide Rock

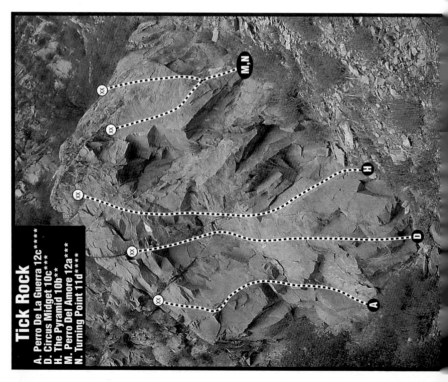

Tick Rock
A. Perro De La Guerra 12c*****
D. Circus Midget 10c****
H. The Pyramid 10b**
M. Perro Del Amore 12a***
N. Turning Point 11d*****

N. Turning Point 11d★★★★

5 bolts to 2 open shuts. Currently the farthest route to the right. Start as for *Perro Del Amore*, but after clipping the first bolt continue climbing the steep right corner to a hard move up and left. From here enjoy fun edge climbing to the top of the face. ➤ Photo page 182.
FA: Louie Anderson, 2002.

Suicide Rock
A. Guinness 6★★

Suicide Rock

Located on the hill up and right from the main formation. It's somewhat involved to get to the base of the route, but it's actually quite a bit more enjoyable than it appears.

A. Guinness 6★★

6 bolts to double bolt anchor. Starts at the right side of the face and climbs through some corners and up the smooth slab above.

G. Swallow's Revenge 9★

8 bolts to 3-bolt anchor. Begin as for *Circus Midget*, but after clipping its 4th bolt go right into a hand crack (optional 1 1/2-2" cam placement here). After clipping the next bolt, traverse left to the anchors.

H. The Pyramid 10b★★

6 bolts to right double bolt anchor. Start climbing up the right prow and after clipping 3 bolts and passing over a small roof, join *Swallow's Revenge*. However after clipping its last bolt continue up and right on easier terrain.

I. Brahm's Chimney 10b★

6 bolts to top 3 closed shuts. Climb *The Pyramid*, but after clipping its last bolt head straight up the chimney/corner to the higher anchors.

J. Original Route 8★

4 bolts, gear: 3 or 4 2" cams to right double bolt anchor. Follow the underclinging flake to the right of *The Pyramid*, finishing on that route.

K. The Blood of Brahm 9(tr)

Start climbing off the big flat rock at the base and wander up the right hand corners passing through a roof low and traversing up and left (following seams) well below the big upper roof. Finishes at the upper 3 closed shuts. Directional anchors in some of the seams would be a good idea if you care to try this one. Be careful of loose rock.

L. Ride the Lightning 11c/d★(tr)

The same beginning as *The Blood of Brahm*, however when that route traverses left this one traverses right to the arete and finishes at the anchors of *Perro Del Amore*.

M. Perro Del Amore 12a★★★

4 bolts to 2 closed shuts. Climb up steep overlaps to a devious slab crux. Very interesting and enjoyable.
FA: Doniel Drazin, Steve Edwards, 2001.

TICK ROCK
Intro: Page 182.

A. Perro De La Guerra 12c★★★★★

7 bolts to 2 open shuts. An excellent route that demands superior footwork and the ability to hold onto some small holds. Begin on *Flying Guillotine* and after clipping its first 2 bolts climb left following the corner. Clip the next 2 bolts of *Flying Guillotine* from the corner and then continue up and left passing 3 more bolts. ➤ Photo page 178.
FA: Doniel Drazin, Steve Edwards, 2001.

B. Flying Guillotine 10c★★★★

7 bolts to shared 2 closed shuts. Climb a short ramp up to the small bulge. Continue up the center of the slab above finishing in a right trending undercling seam (optional 1-1 1/2" cam placement here). ➤ Photo page 183.

C. Holy Crap 9★★★

7 bolts to shared 2 closed shuts. Direct start to *Flying Guillotine*. Climb up the seam to that route's right, passing two bolts before joining it at its 3rd bolt.

D. Circus Midget 10c★★★

7 bolts to shared 3 closed shuts. This route climbs more like granite than sandstone. Climb up the center of the face to a crack under the roof. Jam the crack and turn the roof.

E. Butt Crack 10c★★

10 bolts to top 3 closed shuts. Climb *Circus Midget* and after turning the roof continue past its anchors finishing in the left hand groove. The finish actually takes away from the rest of the route.

F. Right Arete 10c★★

10 bolts to top 3 closed shuts. Same climb as *Butt Crack*, but finish up the right arete/crack after passing the first anchors.

J. Paul Pebble

This little conglomerate boulder lies right on the ocean's edge and is really only climbable at low tide. Surprisingly, it is very solid and has seen a considerable amount of climbing activity over the years. The most popular face is slightly overhung and roughly 20 feet tall, offering climbing

J. Paul Pebble Details

Elevation: Sea level.
Exposure: Varied, sun and shade.
Bouldering: 10+ problems, V0 to V8.
Top-roping: Yes.
Drive From Hwy 1: 0 minutes.
Approach: 5 minute walk.

up a series of water polished cobbles of varying sizes. There are some newer cold shut anchors on top that would suggest some recent top-rope activity and despite the relatively short height, a top-rope (or a few pads and a good spot) is advised due to the poor landings. And no, that white stuff on top of the boulder is not chalk.

The Approach: Map page 180. The boulder is located right below the location of the original J. Paul Getty Museum, at the junction of Pacific Coast Hwy. (1) and Coastline Dr. It's located roughly midway between Sunset Blvd and Topanga Canyon Rd. Another good landmark is a small catamaran "marina" just below the Pacific Coast Hwy. (1), and north of the boulder. Park on the street and scramble down to the base.

Doniel Drazin on **Son of Sam** 11d**** at Black Flower.

See Page 191

See Page 191

Kenny Suh on the vertical slab of **Zodiac** 11c***

Adapted from the U.S.G.S. 1:24,000 Malibu Beach Quadrangle.

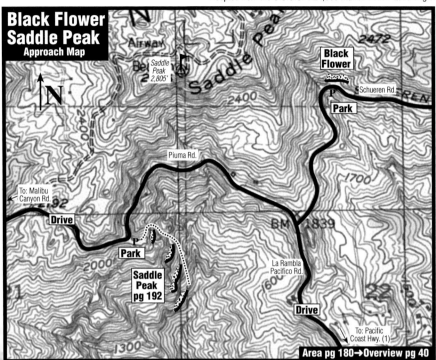

Black Flower

A wonderful little wall, located only 200 feet from the road, that offers some fun climbing. The majority of the routes follow seams and lines of thin edges. All of the routes are a few degrees one side or the other of vertical and climb somewhat similarly. The main exceptions to this are the routes, *Hamburger* and *Do it for Davey,* which climb through a heavily pocketed honeycomb section of rock. The wall is in the shade in the early morning and evening.

Black Flower Details

Elevation: 2,000 ft.
Exposure: South facing.
Sport Climbs: 13 routes, 10d to 12a.
Drive From Hwy 101: 20 minutes.
Drive From Hwy 1: 10 minutes
Approach: 5 minute walk.

The first two routes listed climb what are the most striking lines on the wall. Unfortunately they were not cleaned much prior to their first ascents and are still full of loose rock. The lines have potential and would be very enjoyable if cleaned. There are still quite a few new route options on the left hand, taller portion of the wall. However, any potential new route(s) will require a fair bit of cleaning.

The Approach: *From the Pacific Coast Hwy. (1)* in Malibu, head inland on Las Flores Canyon Rd. (directly opposite Duke's Seafood Restaurant). Follow Las Flores as it winds through the hills. After approximately 5 minutes of driving Las Flores will dead end at La Rambla Pacifico. Turn right here and then right again on the second road you come to (Schueren Rd.). The crag is on the left side of the road and will come into view a minute or so after turning onto Schueren.

From the Ventura Fwy. (101), exit on Las Virgenes Rd. and head west towards the ocean. Shortly after passing the entry for Malibu Creek State Park you will reach a traffic signal at Piuma Rd. Turn left here and head up into the hills. The road twists and turns as you climb up out of Malibu Canyon and cross over a ridge. After passing some scattered homes and a rocky outcropping on your right (Saddle Peak) you will reach Schueren Rd. Turn left here and follow the directions above.

©2003 Maximus Press.

Black Flower
A. Hamburger 11a
B. Do It For Davey 11a
E. Helter Skelter 11d**
I. Black Dahlia 12a****
L. Intimidation 10d**

Black Flower
Intro: Page 189.

A. Hamburger 11a
6 bolts to 2 open shuts. Climb past the first bolt to a ledge. From here, turn a small roof and continue up and left on the heavily pocketed face.
FA: Darshan Etz, Abe, 1997.

B. Do It For Davey 11a
7 bolts to 2 open shuts. Start as for *Hamburger*, but after clipping its first bolt climb up and right following a diagonal line of bolts.
FA: Darshan Etz, Abe, 1997.

C. The Ripper 11a**
3 bolts to 2 open shuts. Climbs the left of two white streaks up a featured face. ➤ Photo page 24.
FA: Louie Anderson, 2002.

D. Night Stalker 11c**
4 bolts to 2 open shuts. This route starts on the right white streak and follows the diagonal seam up and left. Joins *The Ripper* at its last bolt. ➤ Photo page 193.
FA: Louie Anderson, 2002.

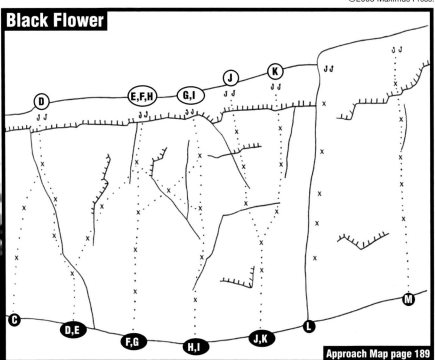

Black Flower

Approach Map page 189

E. Helter Skelter 11d**

 bolts to 2 open shuts. Start as for *Night Stalker*, but after lipping its 1st bolt climb up and right following a seam, and join *Son of Sam* at its last bolt.

A: Louie Anderson, 2002.

. Son of Sam 11d****

 bolts to 2 open shuts. Climb past thin seams to a raverse left at the 3rd bolt. ➤ Photo page 187.

A: Louie Anderson, 2002.

G. Son of Dahlia 12a***

 bolts to 2 open shuts. A link up. Begin on *Son of Sam* nd after clipping its 3rd bolt go right passing 1 ndependent bolt before joining *Black Dahlia* at its last olt.

A: Louie Anderson, 2002.

H. Black Sam 11d***

 bolts to 2 open shuts. A link up. Begin on *Black Dahlia* nd after clipping its 3rd bolt go left passing 1 independent olt before joining *Son of Sam* at its last bolt.

A: Louie Anderson, 2002.

. Black Dahlia 12a****

 bolts to 2 open shuts. Follows a series of thin seams up e vertical black water streak. Often wet for days llowing a rain.

: Louie Anderson, 2002.

J. Serial Driller 11c***

5 bolts to 2 open shuts. Begin climbing at a smooth solution pocket. Climb straight up, passing a band of cobbles, before climbing edges up and left and eventually crossing a roof at the top.

FA: Louie Anderson, 2002.

K. Zodiac 11c***

5 bolts to 2 open shuts. Start as for *Serial Driller*, but after clipping its 2nd bolt traverse right and follow a line of pockets and edges to the top of the wall.

➤ Photo pages 181, 188.

FA: Chris Murray, 2002.

L. Intimidation 10d**

5 bolts to 2 open shuts. Follow the obvious crack line. Could be quite good with a little more traffic.

FA: Darshan Etz, Abe, 1997.

M. Oak Boy 11b

5 bolts to 2 open shuts. This climb is located at the far right side of the wall and follows a slab up to and then over a small roof at the top of the route. The route's accessibility is threatened by the encroaching, adjacent poison oak plants.

FA: Darshan Etz, Abe, 1997.

Saddle Peak

Piuma Rd.

Approach Map page 189

Saddle Peak

Saddle Peak is a pretty amazing collection of formations that spill all the way down the hillside from Piuma Rd. to the creek in the bottom of the canyon far below. Certainly there has been roped climbing and rappelling activities here for some time as evidenced by some of the older anchors found on the many summits. Alan Bell, among others, has developed some bolted lead routes, however it is somewhat difficult to maneuver around the many formations and no specific route information is available to the area's routes.

There is an abundance of rock to be found here and new route activist interested in developing climbs up to the 5.10 level will find a lot of waiting potential. Due to its close proximity to the road, Saddle Peak could become fairly popular with some further development.

The Approach: Map page 189. *From the Pacific Coast Hwy. (1), in Malibu* head inland on Las Flores Canyon Rd. (directly opposite Duke's Seafood Restaurant). Follow Las Flores as it winds through the hills. After approximately 5 minutes of driving Las Flores will dead end at La Rambla Pacifico. Turn right here and continue past Schueren Rd. (La Rambla Pacifico changes to

Saddle Peak Details

Elevation: 2,000 ft.
Exposure: East facing, morning sun.
Sport Climbs: Unknown.
Drive From Hwy 101: 20 minutes.
Drive From Hwy 1: 10 minutes
Approach: 5 to 30 minute scramble.

Piuma Rd. at this point). The collection of large formations across the canyon on your left is Saddle Peak. Park in the dirt turnouts directly above the formations.

From the Ventura Fwy. (101), exit on Las Virgenes Rd. and head west towards the ocean. Shortly after passing the entry for Malibu Creek State Park you will reach a traffic signal at Piuma Rd. Turn left here and head up into the hills. The road twists and turns as you climb up out of Malibu Canyon and cross over the ridge. After passing some scattered homes you will come to some rocky outcroppings on your right. This is Saddle Peak. It's easy to miss when first approaching from this direction, but once you get a short bit past the formations it will be difficult to miss them when looking back. Park in the dirt turnouts directly above the formations.

See Page 190

Steve Edwards on **Night Stalker** 11c** at Black Flower.

Paul Morris and Aaron Brillhart traversing at **The Sandbox** during high water.

See Page 200

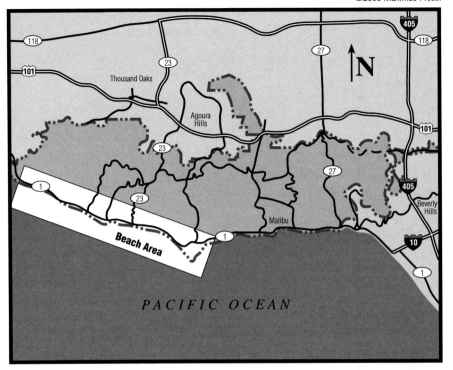

CHAPTER 5

BEACH AREA

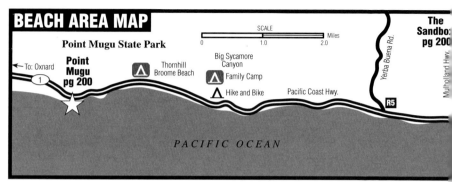

BEACH AREA MAP

SCALE

0   1.0   2.0   Miles

Point Mugu State Park

← To: Oxnard

Point Mugu pg 200

Thornhill Broome Beach

Big Sycamore Canyon

Family Camp

Hike and Bike

Pacific Coast Hwy.

Yerba Buena Rd.

The Sandbox pg 200

Mulholland Hwy.

R5

PACIFIC OCEAN

Josh Conviser on the **Center Route** 8*** at Point Dume.

See Page 199

©2003 Maximus Press.

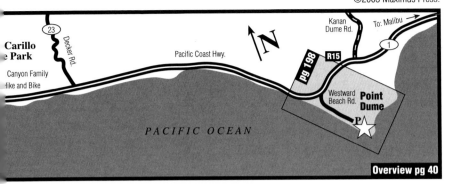

Overview pg 40

Beach Area Basics

N one of the Beach areas can be considered major destinations, how ever each has their core group of dedicated users and all are worthwhile. Of these, Point Dume is by far the most popular and climbers can usually be found climbing here on all but the hottest of weekends.

Getting There

All of the Beach areas are approached from the Pacific Coast Highway (1).

Restaurants

R5. Neptune's Net
Freshly caught seafood.
42505 Pacific Coast Hwy.
☎ 310-457-3095.

R15. Zooma Sushi
Fresh sushi.
29350 Pacific Coast Hwy.
☎ 310-457-4131.

Camping

Leo Carrillo State Park
Canyon Family
Open all year, the fee is $12. Picnic tables, piped water, showers, flush toilets, pets OK, elev. sea level.
☎ 800-444-7275.
Hike and Bike (walk-in)
Open all year, the fee is $1. Picnic tables, piped water, showers, flush toilets, pets OK, elev. sea level.
☎ 805-488-5223.

Big Sycamore Canyon
Family Camp
Open all year, the fee is $12. Picnic tables, piped water, showers, flush toilets, pets OK, elev. sea level.
☎ 800-444-7275.
Hike and Bike (walk-in)
Open all year, the fee is $1. Picnic tables, piped water, showers, flush toilets, no pets, elev. sea level.
☎ 805-488-5223.
Thornhill Broome Beach
Open all year, the fee is $7. Picnic tables, piped water, vault toilets, pets OK, elev. sea level. ☎ 800-444-7275.

Point Dume

This popular beginner's crag lies just steps from the Pacific Ocean, with a base made up of fine white sand. The main slab has a long history of climbing use and has been used as a backdrop for many motion picture and television productions. Due to its close proximity to the ocean, fixed anchors tend to have a short life span. Luckily a group of local climbers seem to replace anchors here on a fairly regular basis. Still, many climbers opt for a toprope on Point Dume's routes. This is easily set up by following the hiker's trail to the summit. Here a large block can be found which is suitable for slinging as a main anchor. Be sure to bring a long piece of webbing or rope for this purpose. There are several bolts to be found on the summit, although their hangers tend to disappear. The climbing on all of the routes tends to follow series of thin, but solid holds up the 50-foot tall, low-angled slab. Be forewarned that the area can get quite crowded with beach goers during the summer months. Please be courteous to all other area users to ensure climbing's continued acceptance in this very public setting.

Point Dume Details

Elevation: Sea level.
Exposure: Northwest facing, afternoon sun.
Sport Climbs: 5 routes, 5.6 to 5.9.
Top-roping: Bring long runners.
Drive From Hwy 1: 5 minutes.
Approach: 5 to 15 minute walk.

©2003 Maximus Press.

Point Dume
Approach Map

Zuma Beach
County Park

To: Point Mugu
Busch Dr.
Bonsall Dr.
To: Malibu
Drive
Pacifc Coast Hwy.
Westward
Beach Rd.
N
Park
P
Malibu
Riviera
P
**Point
Dume**

PACIFIC OCEAN

Area pg 196→Overview pg 40

The Approach: The climbing described below is found at the southeastern end of Zuma Beach County Park, just west of the town of Malibu. From the Pacific Coast Hwy. (1), turn onto Westward Beach Rd. (heading toward the ocean). This street is found just east of the main entry to the County Beach. Follow this road for roughly one mile to a gated payment collection center. Either pay the $5 entry fee and continue 1/2 mile to the parking area at the end of the road, or locate roadside parking before the gate and walk to the end of the road. The climbing is found minutes from the end of the road and is very obvious.

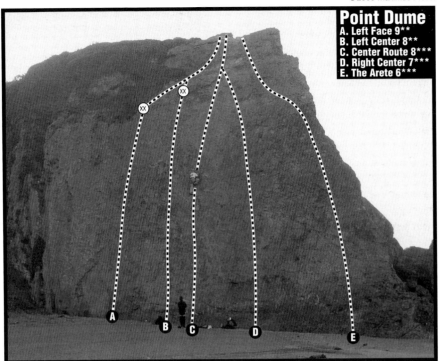

Point Dume
A. Left Face 9**
B. Left Center 8**
C. Center Route 8***
D. Right Center 7***
E. The Arete 6***

Point Dume

A. Left Face 9**
4 bolts to a double ring anchor. Follows the farthest left line of bolts to an anchor located just below the lower bush line.

B. Left Center 8**
4 bolts to a triple ring anchor. Starts five feet left of the central trough and climbs up to anchors located about 20 feet below the summit.

C. Center Route 8***(r)
4 bolts to summit anchor (bring slings). This is the most popular route on the face and climbs the center trough all the way to the summit. Some people opt to traverse left to the lower anchors of the *Left Center* route.
➤ Photo page 196.

D. Right Center 7***(r)
4 bolts to summit anchor (bring slings). Begin climbing 5 feet right of the trough and climb all the way to the top of the slab, sharing the last bolt and final 20-30 feet of climbing with the *Center Route*.

E. The Arete 6***
5 bolts to summit anchor (bring slings). Climbs the right arete and the face just to its left. It takes a bit of route finding to keep the grade at 5.6 and the climbing doesn't necessarily stay right over the bolt line.

West Corridor Routes
Several toprope lines (around 5.10) have been climbed around the corner from *The Arete,* facing the ocean. They all are roughly the same difficulty and climb much steeper terrain than found on the main slab.

The Sandbox

This nice bouldering traverse is unfortunately a little removed from most other climbing options. If this wasn't the case it would surely see more traffic. Located in a creekbed, the traverse climbs on very solid, water-polished rock, using a wide variety of features. It's pretty long and overhung

The Sandbox Details

Elevation: 100 ft..
Exposure: East facing.
Bouldering: 1 problem, V6.
Drive From Hwy 1: 5 minutes.
Approach: 15 minute walk.
Photo: Page 194.

the whole way. The traverse can be climbed in either direction and is probably somewhere around V6 or so in difficulty depending on the sequences used. Although the base of the traverse is usually dry, this creekbed is the main drainage for the area and there may be some water at the left end of the traverse after heavy rains. Photo page 194.

The Approach: Map page 196. The Sandbox can be approached by walking inland from Leo Carillo State Beach through the campground and then up the creek. You will need to pay to park in the campground and this approach will take 20-25 minutes. The traverse is obvious and will be on your right. An alternate and preferred approach can be made by driving inland on Mulholland Hwy. and parking where the road first crosses the creek (1.4 miles from the Pacific Coast Hwy. (1). A trail leaves from the right side turnout and follows the creekbed back towards the beach. There is some poison oak on either side of the trail, but it is easy to avoid if you watch where you're going. The traverse will be reached in about 15 minutes on your left.

Point Mugu

Point Mugu is made up of two separate formations. The most popular offering is a 20 foot tall free standing boulder located in the middle of a large parking turnout, overlooking the ocean. Its north face is slightly overhung and severely fractured, offering several quality crack lines. Most people throw a crash pad down and boulder the cracks, however it's very

Point Mugu Details

Elevation: Sea level.
Exposure: North facing.
Bouldering: 8 problems, 5.8 to 10+.
Top-roping: Bring gear and long runners.
Drive From Hwy 1: 0 minutes.
Approach: 1 minute walk.

easy to set up a top-rope using nuts and small cams on top of the boulder. Other than the lines shown, there are several variation possibilities including some harder options following the thinner seams. The second formation found at Point Mugu is the collection of tall slabs located just north of the boulder. While technically off-limits, they still see somewhat regular climbing activity. No specific route information is presented here as many of the original bolts have deteriorated and several variations exist. Some of the more popular options sport newer bolts, but if you're interested in climbing on the slabs be forewarned that you will probably be relying on a combination of older bolts and small nuts and cams for protection. Some of the rock is actually quite good and some fun climbing can be had on the slabs.

The Approach: Map page 196. Both formations are located right off of the Pacific Coast Hwy. (1), roughly 7 miles west of Yerba Buena Rd. (location of the Neptune's Net seafood restaurant) and 1 mile east of Las Posas Rd. Parking for both formations is in the large ocean side parking turnout adjacent to the boulder.

Point Mugu Slab

Point Mugu Boulder

A. 10+
B. 9
C. 9
D. 9
E. 9
F. 10
G. 10
H. 8

See Page 214

Aaron Brillhart faces a sloping top-out at **Coyote Beach**.

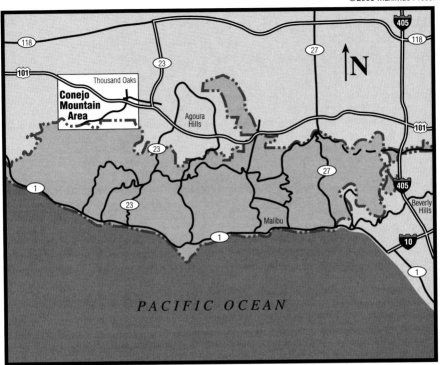

Chapter 6

Conejo Mountain

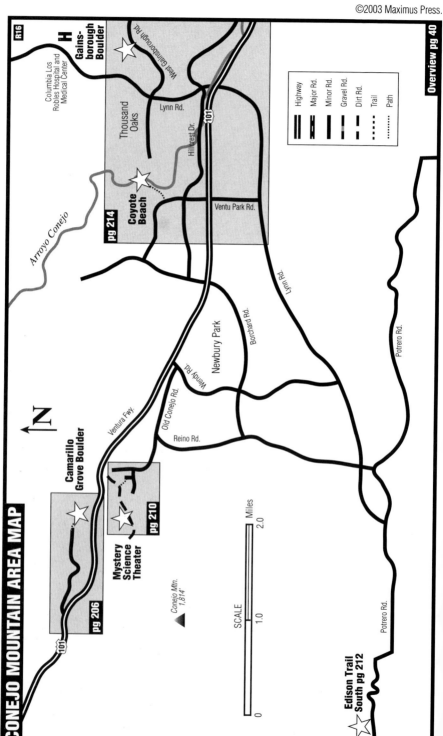

CONEJO MOUNTAIN AREA MAP

Overview pg 40

R16

H
Gains-
borough
Boulder

Columbia Los
Robles Hospital and
Medical Center

West Gainsborough Rd.

Thousand
Oaks

Lynn Rd.

101

Hillcrest Dr.

Arroyo Conejo

pg 214
Coyote
Beach

Ventu Park Rd.

Lynn Rd.

Newbury Park

Borchard Rd.

Potrero Rd.

Wendy Rd.

Old Conejo Rd.

Ventura Fwy.

Reino Rd.

N

Camarillo
Grove Boulder

pg 210
Mystery
Science
Theater

Conejo Mtn.
1,814'

pg 206

101

SCALE

Miles
0   1.0   2.0

Potrero Rd.

Edison Trail
South pg 212

Highway
Major Rd.
Minor Rd.
Gravel Rd.
Dirt Rd.
Trail
Path

CONEJO MOUNTAIN AREA BASICS

The Conejo Mountain Area marks the northern boundary of the Santa Monica Mountains. Located on either side of the Ventura Freeway (101), these areas do not see the traffic that some of the more centrally located areas do, but are still fairly popular with their own "locals." The routes found on top of the ridge at Mystery Science Theater are probably the main attraction here, although the recent activity at Coyote Beach shows the potential of this fine and convenient bouldering venue.

Getting There

All of the Conejo Mountain areas are reached by exiting the Ventura Freeway (101). Each area lies just a few miles from the freeway and all are easily approached using regular surface streets.

Resaurants

R16. Manny's
Family owned Mexican food.
1038 Avenida De Los Arboles.
☎ 805-492-4709

Camping
None Available.

See Page 214

Paul Morris warming up at **Coyote Beach**.

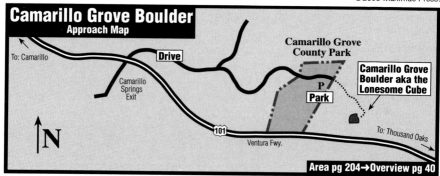

Camarillo Grove Boulder aka the Lonesome Cube

A convenient boulder for fun sessions when your time is limited, the Cube's accessibility has hovered on either side of the legal line since climbers first visited several years ago. Currently there is a sign posted at the beginning of the short approach trail stating that no climbing is allowed. Local climbers are working with the landowners to secure legal access and are hopeful that once again climbers will be welcome to climb here. In the meantime, if the sign is still there when you visit respect the landowner's wishes and continue on to one of the other area bouldering options.

Camarillo Grove Boulder

Elevation: 300 ft.
Exposure: Varied sun and shade
Bouldering: 9 problems, V0 to V5.
Top-roping: Bring runners.
Drive From Hwy 101: 5 minutes.
Approach: 5 to 10 minute walk.

A few of the problems found on the Cube can be a little tall for some people's tastes. If you find this to be the case and want to attempt some of the taller lines, bring your harness, a short rope and some slings; there are bolts located on the boulder's summit over the taller lines. The climbing here is pretty good and is reminiscent of that found up at Mystery Science Theater (no surprise here as the boulder rolled down the hill from its previous home on the same ridge as that area), but on better quality rock. Most of the problems climb heavily pocketed rock that has been cleaned by years of climbing traffic. There is quite a bit of poison oak in the adjacent brush, so watch where you step and stay on the trail. The original names of the problems are long forgotten, but those shown below have become the accepted names. Thank you to the Reverend Speefnarkle.

The Approach: Exit the Ventura Fwy. (101) at the Camarillo Springs Rd. off ramp. Head north and continue on this road as it parallels the freeway. Very shortly you will reach the entrance to Camarillo Grove County Park. Enter the park (you will need to pay a $3.00 fee to park if you decide to stay) and continue to the far side of the park. Walk across the open field and then follow the obvious footpath through the brush and Poison Oak. The Cube is reached about 5-10 minutes after leaving your car.

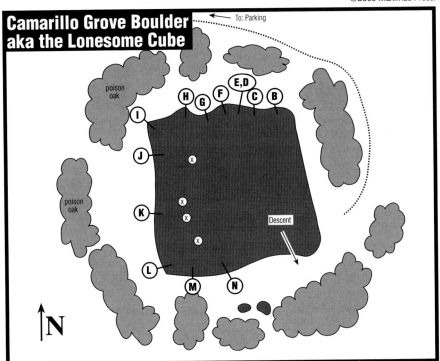

Camarillo Grove Boulder

A. Rotary Salamanders V4***
Traverse the boulder in either direction.

B. Merkenpaste V3*
Sit start and climb the cave, but exit out the left side.

C. Torque Hornet V3*
Sit start and climb out the center of the small cave.

D. Ork Varmit V2**
Sit start and climb out the right side of the cave.

E. Scagglepussy V2**
Start as for *Ork Varmit*, but continue up and right to the top of the boulder.

F. Digihatchet V3***(highball)
Climb straight up using a mono before reaching the crescent shaped edge.

G. Whiffledick V0**(h)
Climb the shallow corner to easier climbing above.

H. Waffle Trumpet V1**(h)
Climbs the right side of the blunt arete. Stay to the left at the top.

I. Too Much Sticky V5*
Sit start and then climb the arete. The sit start is the crux.

J. Hog Scrambler 10b***(tr)
The center of the tallest part of the boulder.

K. Weedmasters III 10c***(tr)
Climbs the tall face, staying near the right edge.

L. Posable Action Hair 10b*(tr)
Stay on the left side and climb the tall arete.

M. Trazloaf 9**(tr)
Climbs the center of the face.

N. Mung Bozo 8*(tr)
The right, lower-angled side of the face.

See Page 211

Annie McMillan on **Dues Servomachina** 11d**.

Mystery Science Theater aka Conejo Mountain

The development of Mystery Science Theater (MST) as a sport climbing area coincided with the publication of the now-defunct regional magazine, *Allez*, and most of the routes were bolted by those behind the publication and their circle of friends. The area en-

Mystery Science Theater

Elevation: 1,000 ft.
Exposure: Varied sun and shade.
Sport Climbs: 20 routes, 5.6 to 12d.
Top-roping: Bring long runners.
Drive From Hwy 101: 5 minutes.
Approach: 15 to 45 minute walk.

joyed a fair amount of popularity due to the instant availability of route information in the magazine (and the lack of other options back then) and the convenient fire road access. At the time of development MST was approached by a parking area much closer to the routes, resulting in a quicker and easier approach than what is available now. Unfortunately, climbers were not the only ones frequenting the area and the story goes that some imbecile decided it would be fun to climb on the electrical towers found along the ridgeline. After his electrocution death, the approach road was blocked. With the development of other sport climbing options in the Santa Monicas, and with the now longer approach, MST's popularity has dwindled.

The climbing at MST is found on short, individual formations on rock that is for the most part sound. While it's unlikely that anyone climbing here will rave about the overall quality, there are in fact some very fine routes interspersed within the rest of the area's offerings, and a trip for local climbers would more than likely be worthwhile and enjoyable.

The Approach: Map page 210. Exit the Ventura Fwy. (101) at the Wendy Dr. off ramp. Head south and immediately turn right onto Old Conejo Rd. Just after passing Reino Rd. on your left you will come to the Pepper Tree Playfield (also on your left). Park in the playfield parking lot (there is no legal street parking) and then walk back out onto Old Conejo Rd. and follow it to your left (away from the direction you came). Continue following this road as it turns to the right until you come to Vista Conejo and the entry to the Vallecito Mobile Home Park. Enter the park and then turn right on the first street (La Lomita). Shortly after making this turn you will see a sign on your left cautioning about rattlesnakes and mountain lions (photo page 9). Head up onto the hillside near this sign and follow faint trails until you intersect with the fire road above. Go left on this road and you will reach the main area on your right in a matter of minutes.

An Alternate approach is to continue on Old Conejo Rd. (past the mobile home park) to the end of the road. Find your way to the other side of the chain link fence and follow the fire road uphill to the main area.

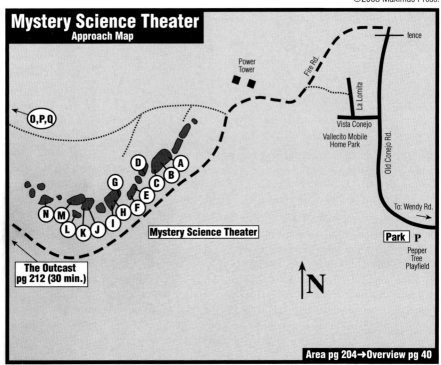

Mystery Science Theater
Approach Map

fence

Power Tower

Fire Rd.

O,P,Q

La Lomita

Vista Conejo
Vallecito Mobile
Home Park

Old Conejo Rd.

D
A
G
C
B
E
N
M
I
H
F
L
K
J

Mystery Science Theater

To: Wendy Rd.

Park P

Pepper
Tree
Playfield

**The Outcast
pg 212 (30 min.)**

N

Area pg 204→Overview pg 40

Mystery Science Theater
C. High School Big Shot 7*
F. Dues Servomachina 11d**
I. The Beginning of the End 10c***

XX

XX

F

XX

C

I

Mystery Science Theater

Intro: page 209. The routes are listed right to left as they are approached on the fire road.

A. A Whole New Day O' Rockclimin' 8

3 bolts to double bolt anchor.
missing bottom bolt
TR Feb 5 2006
FA: Binky Greene, 1994.

B. Racket Girls 9

3 bolts to double bolt anchor.
missing bottom bolt
TR Feb 5
FA: Binky Greene, 1994.

C. High School Big Shot 7*

3 bolts to double bolt anchor. Climbs the steep arete on big holds. *Andrew lead Feb 5, 2006* *2006*
FA: Dave Scott, 1994.

D. Torgo 6

The bolts and anchors from this route have been removed, so if you choose to climb it you'll be forced to solo it or rig up a top-rope.
FA: Dave Scott, 1994.

E. Servo the Bloodletter 11c*(tr)

Climbs the face to the right of *Dues Servomachina*. Clip the one directional bolt to eliminate the swing.
FA: Steve Edwards, 1993.

F. Dues Servomachina 11d**

4 bolts to double bolt anchor. Pull through a difficult pocket move down low and continue up thin holds to the top. It's easier to clip the anchors from the holds out left.
➤ Photo page 208.
FA: Jason Houston, 1993.

G. Are You Happy in Your Work? 10a(tr)

Top-ropes the right face, but try not to fall low as you'll be in for a nasty swing.
FA: Jason Houston, 1993.

H. I Accuse My Parents 10a**

3 bolts to double bolt anchor. Ascend the center of the face on moves that aren't as runout as they look.
FA: Jason Houston, 1993.

I. The Beginning of the End 10c***

5 bolts to double chain anchor. A great route that climbs the left arete via fun moves on good holds.
➤ Photo this page, page 213.
FA: Steve Edwards, 1993.

J. Daddy-O 10c**

4 bolts to double bolt anchor.
FA: Scott Buchanan, 1994.

K. Manos, Hands of Fate 10a(tr)

Climbs the arete left of *Daddy-O*.
FA: Scott Buchanan, 1994.

L. The Infinity of the Depths of a Man's Mind 10c

3 bolts to double bolt anchor. Good rock, but the name may be longer than the route.
FA: Binky Greene, 1994.

M. Push the Button, Frank 8(tr)

Climbs the long slab. *No easy anchors at top, Dirty long (15-20m) static*
FA: Steve Edwards, 1994.

N. Follow Your Bliss 11b**

4 bolts to double bolt anchor. Very thin and sustained climbing up the left prow of the face.
FA: Stuart Ruckman, 1992.

O. Unnamed 10c*

3 bolts to double bolt anchor. This lone route climbs up the face on pretty good rock.

The following routes are on the tall wall overlooking the Ventura Fwy. (101). Be careful where you step as the area around these routes is loaded with poison oak. There is potential here for additional routes, however any development would require some clearing of the area's poison oak to access the walls.

P. Alien From L.A. 10(tr)

Face.

Q. Oh Kathy, My Kathy 11a/b(tr)

Climb over the prow.

Jamie Hays on **The Beginning of the End** 10c***.

The Outcast

Mystery Science Theater Intro: Page 210. A little removed from the main area, but well worth the extra walk if the grades are within your reach. This large boulder offers routes that are longer and steeper than those found at the main area. Continue walking along the fire road passing a few more sets of power towers until you reach the boulder located behind a pair of towers. The routes are on the back of the boulder as you approach it. Go around the left side to the routes in order to avoid the poison oak growing to the right of the boulder. The walk should take approximately 30 minutes from the main area.

The Outcast

Approach Map page 210

R. Junk Bonds 12d★★

7 bolts to 2 open shuts. Climb the clean left face passing a low, difficult crux to reach more enjoyable 5.11 climbing on the upper half.
FA: Stuart Ruckman, 1992.

S. The Outcast 12a★★★

6 welded cold shut bolts to 2 open shuts. Straight up the center of the face, using somewhat sharp holds.
FA: Stuart Ruckman, 1992.

T. Cowgirl Paradise 11c★★★

6 bolts to 2 open shuts located on the ledge above the route. Probably the best of the three. Climb the right face using several fun pockets and blocky jugs.
FA: Stuart Ruckman, 1992.

Edison Trail South

High on the ridge over Channel Islands University (which used to be Camarillo Mental Hospital) lies a group of small formations. Three routes can be found on the largest face. The quality of the routes is decent, but the approach is long and overgrown. Unless you are trying to "check off"

Edison Trail South Details

Elevation: 500 ft.
Exposure: South facing.
Sport Climbs: 3 routes, 5.8 to 11b.
Drive From Hwy 101: 20 minutes.
Approach: 30 minute hike.

all the area routes you might want to opt for Mystery Science Theater instead.

The Approach: Map page 204. The formation is approached off of West Potrero Rd. From the Ventura Fwy. (101) exit at the Wendy Dr. off ramp. Head south and make an immediate right turn onto Old Conejo Rd. Follow this road to Reino Rd. where you will turn left. Continue on Reino Rd. up into the hills until you come to an intersection with Lynn Rd. Turn right here and go 3.6 miles before looking for a small service road on the north side of the road (adjacent to the Potrero Valley Ranch). Park on the side of the road and walk down this service road for about 100 yards. A small trail will leave the service road on your right side and head up towards the ridgeline. Follow this trail to the obvious formation.

Edison Trail South

Edison Trail South

Jamie Hays on **The Beginning of the End** 10c***.

See Page 211

This crag can also be approached by exiting the Ventura Fwy. (101) below the Camarillo Grade at the Lewis Rd. off ramp. Head towards the ocean until you come to an intersection with Potrero Rd. Turn left here and go 1.9 miles before looking for the service road described above, on your left.

Routes are listed left to right as you are looking at the face.

A. Hubba Bubba 8**

4 bolts to double bolt anchor. Climbs the left side of the face.
FA: Dave Scott, 1995.

B. Ain't No Disco 11b**

4 bolts to double bolt anchor. Turns the small roof in the center of the face.
FA: Dave Scott, 1995.

C. Rookie Arena 9*

5 bolts to double bolt anchors. Start on *Ain't No Disco*, but after clipping its first bolt traverse right and then up.
FA: Dave Scott, 1995.

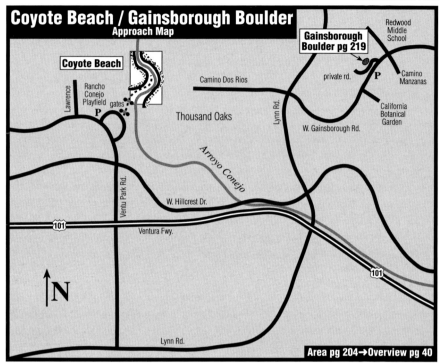

Coyote Beach / Gainsborough Boulder
Approach Map

Gainsborough Boulder pg 219

Redwood Middle School

Coyote Beach

Rancho Conejo Playfield

Lawrence

gates

P

Camino Dos Rios

private rd.

P

Camino Manzanas

Lynn Rd

Thousand Oaks

California Botanical Garden

W. Gainsborough Rd.

Arroyo Conejo

Ventu Park Rd.

W. Hillcrest Dr.

101

Ventura Fwy.

101

↑N

Lynn Rd.

Area pg 204→Overview pg 40

Coyote Beach

Another of the hidden gems in the Santa Monicas. Coyote Beach lies in the Arroyo Conejo Greenbelt. This small section of open space lies right in the midst of block after block of Thousand Oaks and Newbury Park homes. Minutes after leaving the car you can be enjoying one of the many bouldering traverses or working out the moves on a bulging "up" problem. There's flowing water here year-round and the sound of its cascades allows you to easily forget just how urban the place really is.

Coyote Beach Details

Elevation: 600 ft.
Exposure: Varied.
Bouldering: 40+ problems, VB to V10.
Drive From Hwy 101: 5 minutes.
Approach: 5 to 20 minute walk.

Coyote Beach is somewhat of a complicated area. While there is certainly plenty of quality rock to be found here, some of the best rock lies over bad and/or water landings limiting the full development of the area's options. Many of the more popular zones have obvious traverses and problems, but to fully appreciate the potential requires an open mind and a willingness to create and enjoy eliminates. There is one incredibly short route that has been bolted here already, but it's a joke and wouldn't be worth bringing your harness and rope even if it was right by the car. Further bolting is not encouraged and would more than likely create access issues. Realize that there are homes that back up to the arroyo on either side and that yelling and radios can easily be heard. Be respectful of the adjacent homeowners and keep loud noises to an absolute minimum.

The rock is a water polished and fine grained sandstone that is very friendly on the skin. The majority of the usable features are either slopers or solution pockets varying from monos to huge huecos. Although the area is known for its traverses, there are also some very enjoyable bulges and sloping topout problems. A pad can be used in some areas, however many of the bases would be difficult to protect with one and maneuvering around the area with a pad could be somewhat problematic. The best advice would be to forgo the pad on your initial visit and then to bring one on subsequent visits when you are more familiar with the area.

There are several established problems and you will no doubt see a fair amount of chalk when you visit, but due to the lack of published information and the presence of conflicting information where it is available, no specific problem information will be addressed here (other than showing some of the more popular zones and traverses).

The Approach: Exit the Ventura Fwy. (101) at the Ventu Park Dr. off ramp. Head north, crossing West Hillcrest Dr., and continue until you reach Rancho Conejo Playfield on your right (just as the road turns to the left). Park in the playfield parking lot and find the gate at the far right corner of the lot. Walk around the gate and follow the dirt road down into the arroyo. Continue past the second gate and follow the dirt and concrete path as it winds into the rock walled arroyo. The first bouldering is found immediately after the arroyo takes a sharp turn to the left and continues for roughly 1/4 to 1/2 mile.

©2003 Maximus Press.

Coyote Beach
Bouldering Map

↑N

waterfall

waterfall

The Cave

Main Area

Crouching Tiger

← To: Parking

Arroyo Conejo

Approaching the **Main Area** at Coyote Beach.

Coyote Beach
Crouching Tiger Traverse

Coyote Beach
Main Area

Aaron Brillhart bouldering at **The Cave**, Coyote Beach.

Coyote Beach
The Cave
A. 2 Bolt Lead 10d
B. Rail Traverse V4**

Paul Morris nearing the end of the **Rail Traverse** V4****.

Gainsborough Boulder

Traverse Boulder

Main Boulder

Gainsborough Boulder

This lonely little cluster of boulders is somewhat pathetic, but sees activity from local climbers looking for a quick diversion. There are a handful of somewhat committing problems (V2-V6) on the main boulder and a decent overhung traverse (V1-V2) on the upper boulder. Really only worthwhile due to its convenience and the fact that climbers probably drive right by these boulders on a regular basis.

The Approach: Map page 214. Exit the Ventura Fwy. (101) at the Lynn Rd. off ramp. Head north until you reach West Gainsborough Rd. Turn right here and park on the shoulder just after passing the entry to the California Botanical Garden on your right. The boulders can be seen on your left side set back just a short ways from the road.

Gainsborough Boulder

Elevation: 800 ft.
Exposure: Varied.
Bouldering: 10 problems, V1 to V6.
Drive From Hwy 101: 5 minutes.
Approach: 5 minute walk.

Rachel Lincoln and Mark Stuver of Project Bandaloop on the Java Wall. *Thomas Cavanagh Photo.*

Just another of the many unclimbed formations in the backcountry.

CHAPTER 7

APPENDIX

ROUTES BY RATING

5

❏ Ramp Route   59
❏ Simple Gully   70

6

❏ Torgo   211

6**

❏ Golden Years (1st pitch) 87
❏ Guinness   185
❏ Serpent (1st pitch)   87

6***

❏ Arete   199

7

❏ B.E.M. (Booger Eatin' Moron)   97

7*

❏ High School Big Shot   211
❏ Rockhopper   87

7**

❏ Head Wound (1st pitch)   87
❏ Xanadu   55

7***

❏ Right Center   199
❏ Righteous Babe (1st pitch)   87

8

❏ Blackjack (3rd pitch)   87
❏ Push the Button, Frank (tr)   211
❏ Whole New Day O' Rockclimin'   211

8*

❏ Little Giant   55
❏ Mung Bozo (tr)   207
❏ Original Route   185

8**

❏ Black Crack   89
❏ Classic Malibu Face (tr) 137
❏ Game Boy   55
❏ Hubba Bubba   213
❏ Left Center   199

8***

❏ Center Route   199
❏ Righteous Babe (2nd pitch)   87

8****

❏ Chopping Block   139
❏ Dirty Deeds   87

9

❏ Blood of Brahm (tr)   185
❏ Dead Rats   145
❏ Grape Ape (tr)   135
❏ Heirloom   53
❏ Junk Ramp   145
❏ Racket Girls   211

9*

❏ Bushwacked   57
❏ Junior   55
❏ Morning Glory   57
❏ Power Ranger   153
❏ Rookie Arena   213
❏ Swallow's Revenge   185

9**

❏ Bubba   157
❏ K-2   141
❏ Left Face   199
❏ Medusa   97
❏ Powder Puff Girls   153
❏ Satin Shoes   99
❏ Trazloaf (tr)   207

9***

❏ Blacklisted   89
❏ Golden Years (2nd pitch) 87
❏ Holy Crap   185
❏ Miss Pacman   55
❏ Scarab   150
❏ Watermark   87

9****

❏ Head Wound (2nd pitch)   87

10a

❏ Are You Happy in Your Work? (tr)   211
❏ Christmas Pump (tr)   135
❏ Manos, Hands of Fate (tr)   211
❏ Reverb   57

10a*

❏ B-line   57

10d**

10d***

10d****

10d/11a*****

11a

11a*

11a**

11a***

11a****

11a*****

11a/b

11a/b**

11a/b***

11b

11b*

11b**

11b***

❏ Ground Zero	145
❏ Joy Rush	109
❏ New Release	139
❏ Tuxedo	99
❏ Up Chuck	94

12a***

❏ Death Before Decaf	59
❏ Energy	89
❏ French Roast	59
❏ Geezer	79
❏ Gorilla of My Dreams (tr)	135
❏ Gorilla Warfare (tr)	135
❏ Jolt	89
❏ Outcast	212
❏ Perro Del Amore	185
❏ Son of Dahlia	191
❏ Whippersnapper	79

12a****

❏ Black Dahlia	191
❏ Calm	62
❏ Conspiracy	116
❏ Immaculate Annihilation	85
❏ Pretty in Pink	67
❏ Stain	61

12a*****

❏ Drifter	151
❏ Immaculate	85

12a/b****

❏ Urban Struggle	145

12b

❏ Spam	79

12b*

❏ Dean's Route	77
❏ Pluto	97
❏ Super Tick	85

12b**

❏ Caviar	99
❏ Hole Patrol	145
❏ Monkey Business (tr)	135
❏ Psychoholic	69

12b***

❏ Carnivore	79
❏ Code Blue	122
❏ Dipstick	55
❏ Lucky Charms	74
❏ Obituary	159
❏ Pink Flamingo	67

❏ Super Mac	85
❏ Trailer Trash	157
❏ Whizbang	95

12b****

❏ Buddha Belly	75
❏ Daily Grind	59
❏ Daily Java	59
❏ Hijacked	83
❏ Piledriver	109
❏ Spontaneous Wisdom	77

12b/c**

❏ Brain Stew	109
❏ Joy Stew	109

12b/c***

❏ Awakening	77

12c

❏ Toxeth Walk	145

12c**

❏ Darkest Hour	145
❏ Lunge or Plunge (tr)	137
❏ Malibu Swinger (tr)	161

12c***

❏ Choptop	61
❏ Eraserhead	107
❏ Grunt	107
❏ Johnny Can't Lead	145
❏ Meditation Station	77
❏ Stink Finger	145
❏ Swamp Thing	149

12c****

❏ Booty	75
❏ Meager and Weak	67
❏ Perro De La Guerra	185

12c*****

❏ Shiva	75

12c/d**

❏ Apes of Wrath (tr)	135
❏ Brave New Grunt	107
❏ Cross Dresser (tr)	161
❏ Stun Gun	145

12d**

❏ Bloodsucker	123
❏ Brutal Bypass	85
❏ Chubby	107
❏ Grunt Plus	107

See Page 116

Doniel Drazin on **Eye to the Sky** 11b**** at The Lookout.

BOULDER PROBLEMS BY RATING

VB

❏ Eve *	175
❏ Malibu Lieback **	171
❏ Peakbagger *	175
❏ Soul Power *	166
❏ Soul Sister **	166
❏ Violator *	166

V0-

❏ Adam's Rib *	175
❏ Groove Armada *	175
❏ Sole Food **	166

V0

❏ Bigger Than Big **	173
❏ Finger Function *	177
❏ Freebase *	169
❏ Gadzooks *	165
❏ Flat Funk **	172
❏ Hot Rod *	165
❏ Jumping Jack *	172
❏ Junkie **	169
❏ Phat Albert *	165
❏ Test Tube **	173
❏ Whiffledick **	207

V0+

❏ Buzz Saw **	169
❏ Crater Arete **	177
❏ Flydaddy **	169
❏ Luckyman **	177
❏ Scoop **	176
❏ Simple Simon *	172
❏ Sugar Daddy *	166

V1-

❏ Enforcer **	166

V1

❏ Holey Moley *	165
❏ Knob Job *	165
❏ Lost in Space **	169
❏ Massive**	173
❏ Mickey Mantle **	175
❏ Scoop Traverse ***	176
❏ Shell Arete *	172
❏ Slaphappy ***	175
❏ Small Fry *	172
❏ Street Legal **	165
❏ Waffle Trumpet **	207

V1+

❏ Apparatus **	176
❏ Bouldering for Dollars **	171
❏ Cobble in a Dish **	169
❏ Depatment of Water and Power (DWP) *	171
❏ Redstone *	169
❏ Slapstick **	175

V2

❏ Barracuda ***	169
❏ Butterball **	176
❏ Crocodile Rock *	171
❏ Flyweenakiss ***	169
❏ Friction **	172
❏ Giant Steps Unfold **	171
❏ Hot Mama ***	173
❏ Kingpin **	169
❏ Like Glass **	175
❏ Intimidation **	176
❏ Locals Only **	177
❏ Ork Varmit **	207
❏ Phat Cat **	165
❏ Pipe Dream *	169
❏ Powder Edge **	165
❏ Power to the People **	173
❏ Rebel Yell *	173
❏ Revolt **	173
❏ Rock Lobster **	169
❏ Scagglepussy **	207
❏ Tension **	173
❏ Tie-Dye *	177
❏ Under the Gun *	176
❏ Underdog *	173

V2+

❏ Flake and Bake **	173
❏ Fraidy Cat **	171
❏ Islands in the Stream ****	177
❏ Junkyard Dog **	172
❏ Oasis **	171

V3-

❏ Crawdaddy *	169

V3

❏ Balancing Act ***	175
❏ Blockhead **	165
❏ Digihatchet ***	207
❏ Drug Lord ****	169
❏ El Diablo *****	173
❏ Fear Factor ***	171
❏ Flyboy **	173
❏ Great Divide ***	173

See Page 83

Clint Weber on **Crash and Burn** 12d***** at Echo Cliffs.

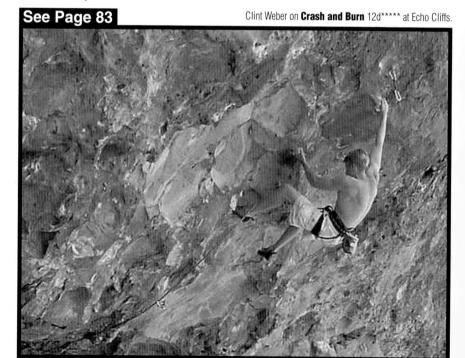

FIXEhardware

Ring Anchor

New # 714.434.9166

fixehardware@mindspring.com

www.fixeusa.com

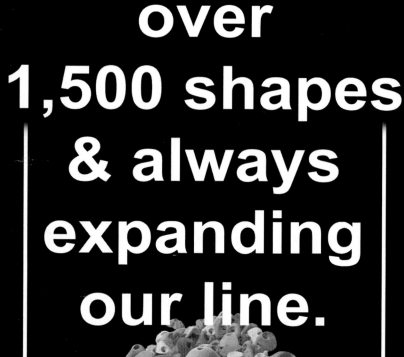

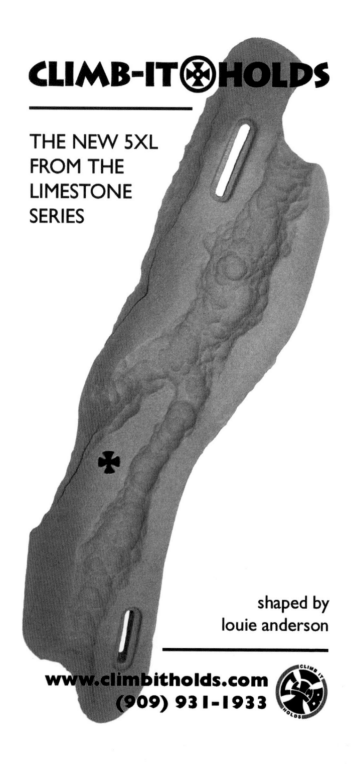

INDEX

See Page 59

Aron Couzens on **Java** 11d***** at Echo Cliffs.

©Perri Nguyen Photo.

ABOUT THE AUTHOR

L ouie Anderson has been climbing since the age of eight, having been introduced to the sport through a friend of his father. In the years since, he has enjoyed several different aspects of the sport, from bouldering to big walls to overseas sport climbing. Louie's main interest lies in new routes. Whether it be hunting for new areas or establishing new routes at existing areas, this aspect of our sport is what fuels his motivation. Since the discovery of Echo Cliffs in 1994, the Santa Monica Mountains have grabbed and maintained Louie's attention to the exclusion of almost all other areas. Many of the routes in this guide were established by him and he has plans in store for several additional routes and areas for the years to come.

Aside from his new route related labors, Louie works as a Project Manager for a General Contractor and has his own climbing wall construction company. He also designs artificial climbing holds for several companies. Louie is happily married to his wife of 13 years, Carla, and the pair have two daughters: Kayla and Madison, ages 9 and 6. The Anderson family lives in a rural area of Orange County, California in a house that they built themselves.

ABOUT MAXIMUS PRESS

Maximus Press was inadvertently launched in 1990 with the publication of the pamphlet "<u>Owens River Gorge Climbs</u>". Garage-style in appearance, this publication was nevertheless, accurate, concise and easy to use. Thirteen years later after considerable improvements, Maximus Press continues to strive to produce the most useful and state-of-the-art guidebooks possible. The knowledge base of our expert authors and editorial staff comes from years of experience climbing, exploring and living in California. You can count on our commitment to deliver high-quality books.

I grew up in the Santa Monica Mountains. This is where I began hiking and scrambling in the natural world. I was always intrigued by the amazing rock formations scattered about these mountains. The Mediterranean climate and beautiful wilderness setting make the Santa Monica Mountains a fantastic Southern California resource. So it was with great pleasure that I agreed to work with local activist Louie Anderson on this project. Enjoy!

—Marty Lewis
Publisher

The Maximus Press editorial staff compiling a quality guidebook.

Bishop, Ca. production facilities.

Another shipment of books coming your way.

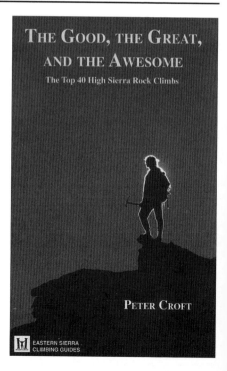

OWENS RIVER GORGE CLIMBS

by Marty Lewis

EASTERN SIERRA CLIMBING GUIDES VOL. 1

June 2000 - 9th Edition
136 pages - $19.00
ISBN 0-9676116-2-8

Featuring 600 fantastic climbs at California's premiere sport climbing area.

- **Negress Wall**
- **Social Platform**
- **Great Wall of China**
- **Eldorado Roof**
- **Dilithium Crystal**
- **Gorgeous Towers**

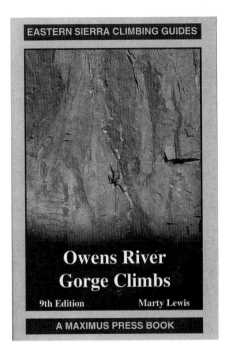

BISHOP AREA ROCK CLIMBS

by John Moynier and Marty Lewis

EASTERN SIERRA CLIMBING GUIDES VOL. 3

December 1999 - 2nd Edition
104 pages - $13.00
ISBN 0-9676116-1-X

A Guidebook to Cragging and Bouldering in the Bishop, California Area

- **Buttermilk Boulders**
- **Little Egypt**
- **Cardinal Pinnacle**
- **Happy Boulders**
- **Pine Creek**
- **Rock Creek**

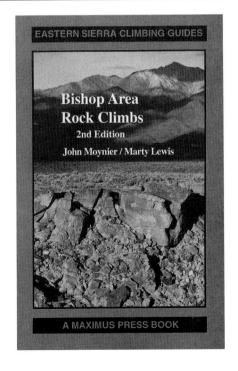